THE CHANGING FACE OF THEOLOGY

THE
CHANGING FACE
OF
THEOLOGY

PATRICK FANNON, S.M.M.

THE BRUCE PUBLISHING COMPANY / *Milwaukee*

IMPRIMI POTEST:
>   WILFRED JUKKA, S.M.M.
>   Provincialis in Anglia

NIHIL OBSTAT:
>   JOHN A. SCHULIEN, S.T.D.
>   Censor librorum

IMPRIMATUR:
>   ✝ WILLIAM E. COUSINS
>   Archbishop of Milwaukee
>   June 3, 1968

The Nihil obstat and imprimatur are a declaration that a book or pamphlet is considered to be free from doctrinal or moral error. It is not implied that those who have granted the Nihil obstat and Imprimatur agree with the contents, opinions, or statements expressed.

Library of Congress Catalog Card Number: 68–8284

Foreword

The present book is the outcome of a series of articles in the English *Clergy Review* of 1967. They were designed to give in capsule form to the readers of that journal, clerical and lay — theology is too serious a business to be left only to clerics — some knowledge of the main thrust of post-conciliar theology.

The series was organized along the lines of the plan governing most of our standard textbooks of theology so that even a lingering acquaintance with such manuals and college courses could serve as a departure point for what may seem to many to be an expedition into the unknown. *Hic sunt leones*: the warning of the old Roman cartographers, calling legionaries back to base, need not, however, be applied to these pages. An attempt is being made to discuss issues which have achieved some degree of general acceptance in current theological debate.

On account of this clearly defined object of the series, much of the intricacy involved in that debate has been left intentionally to the "Suggestions for further reading" appended to each chapter. On the other hand, I have not been content merely to list the present changes in theological perspectives. This would look dangerously like tabloid theology where the value of theological assertions is appraised in terms of would-be shock therapy. Some discussion was called for to give depth and dimension to the topics dealt with.

It may come as a surprise to some that specific chapters on christology and mariology find no place in this book. But it must be recognized that modern theology has, in the case of christology, exhibited scarcely any development (admittedly, there is the vision of Teilhard de Chardin of

v

the cosmic Christ, but much more work is to be done before his christology can be fully assessed). Mariology, on the
other hand, presents us with the unusual phenomenon of
theological elephantiasis. Under Pius XII it reached the
limits of overdevelopment, limits which were necessarily
inherent in the course it was pursuing. It had become almost an autonomous discipline, in isolation from the main-
stream of theology; it was employing an exegesis that was
pietistic and hopeful rather than informed; it was indis-
criminate in its use of tradition. Cold, critical conciliar
winds put an end to an era. But the Council also opened
new perspectives and perhaps, when the more pressing needs
of the Council have been met, we may look forward to a
renewal in mariology.

I have already referred to reading lists given at the end
of each chapter. Realizing that specialists would be able to
provide their own bibliographies for the subjects dealt with, I
have confined those book lists to the more accessible and
manageable modern studies. Obviously they are only one
man's choice, but I have tried to make them as representative as possible. In the shadow of the Council there have
been numerous surveys, evaluations, probes from both Catholic and Protestant scholars, and one must of necessity be
selective.

My thanks are due to the editor of the *Clergy Review*,
Fr. Michael Richards, for his kind permission to publish
this material in the present form. It was an opportunity
for revision and rewriting. I have added subtitles. I should
also like to thank the many, clergy and laity, who have
expressed their appreciation of the series during its publica-
tion. I await with much interest the comments from North
America.

PATRICK FANNON, S.M.M.

Contents

Contents

THE CHANGING FACE OF THEOLOGY

1. The Forces at Work From the Modern World

CHANGING THE STATUS QUO

Time was when Catholic teaching in seminaries, in schools, and from pulpits followed a uniform and stabilized pattern that enjoyed all the security of a well-tried system. You knew what you had to preach, teach, and learn. But with the Copernican revolution in theology of the past few years, with the questions raised in post-conciliar probes, with newspaper reports of doctrinal alarums and excursions abroad, there is doubt now and confusion among many. The sally of Ronald Knox, some fifty years ago, against the upheaval caused by the Anglican essays in *Foundations*, finds an echo in innumerable minds today:

> So, Freedom reign'd; so Priests, dismay'd by naught,
> Thought what they pleas'd, and mention'd what they
>   thought . . .
> Till men began for some Account to call,
> What we believ'd, or why believ'd at all? . . .
> When suave Politeness, temp'ring bigot Zeal,
> Corrected, "I believe," to "One does feel."

There were those, consequently, who rejoiced at the 1966 Letter of Cardinal Ottaviani calling for episcopal investi-

1

gation on a ten-point syllabus of nascent deviations. Others, however, taking to heart the advice of 1 Thessalonians 5:21 to "try everything," have erected chains of theological cafeterias where the gourmand is more catered to than the gourmet. As to our modern *anawim*, the poor of Yahweh, the comfortable old overcoat that was their faith and devotions shows signs of turning into a hairshirt. Drifting on a cloud of unknowing, they leave all to the silent touches of time — *solvitur vivendo*.

Yet, despite undeniable excesses from both right and left fringe groups in theology; despite, too, the uncertainty of many, the nostalgia of the pious, it has to be recognized that the personal call of the Church to renewal and reformation must inevitably introduce changes, often of a somewhat disconcerting nature. Transitional periods are never noted for their comfort. For the Church (as Newman pointed out for all organic realities) to live is to change, and to be perfect is to have changed often. Earlier periods had seen the triumphant transcendency of the Church extolled, but there is more appreciation now of her incarnational aspect by which she realizes more and more her own nature by experiencing her action in and for the world of men. In time, in history, in the affairs of this world, she must not remain static but must develop and grow. Mankind itself is continually manifesting a pattern of change that the Church, the *sacramentum mundi*, the sign of God's presence in the world, cannot ignore.

Hence, if biblical, liturgical, ecumenical scholars have been concerned to uncover features of the Church's authentic self, if philosophers have probed the findings of world thought to erect a platform on which the Church and the world can meet in dialogue, if the Church itself in Council has had to revise its understanding of its status vis-à-vis other Christian communities, non-Christian religions, the temporal order — all this has not been the work of maverick enthusiasts, impatient of tradition and received ideas. Counter Reform polemics, the blanket condemnation of secularism in the past century, the oppressive measures and attitude toward Protestant liberalism, the tolerance (at least) of an individualistic *devotio moderna* — defend these how we will from past historical circumstances, they diverted energies in the Church which can presently be better organized toward discovering the more profound role the Church should have among the mankind she is here to save. If barnacles must be scraped from the bark of Peter, it is unavoidable that here and there a plank will suffer. But the workmen are committed to making her seaworthy, not to foundering her.

A glance at the sixteen documents from Vatican II can give us an indication of which forces have been behind this process of renewal. We can notice a growing self-awareness of the *Church* (documents on the Church, Revelation, Liturgy, Eastern Catholics, Bishops, Priests, Religious, Laity, Christian Education); then, recognition of other *Christians* — churches and ecclesial communities (Ecumenism); lastly, confrontation with the *World* (Church in the Modern World, Missionary Activity, non-Christian Religions, Religious Freedom, Communications). It must be evident that many concerns and perspectives of the various documents overlap: chapters in earlier drafts became documents in their own right, e.g. "Non-Christian Religions" and "Religious Freedom" were originally chapters four and five of the draft on Ecumenism (which also included treatment of the separated Eastern Churches); "Ecumenism" itself was previously part of the draft on the "Church"; "Missions" is something of a continuation of the document on the Church.

For purposes of clarity, then, we can isolate three forces at work on the changing face of our theology: (1) dialogue with the world; (2) dialogue with other Christian bodies; (3) dialogue within the Church. Here we shall examine the first of these three forces, offering a sketch which must be confined to the primary colors; the pastel shades of opinion are too numerous and often too undefinable to be included on a canvas designed for the eyes of the interested amateur.

We may well begin by acknowledging (despite some tendencies of our ascetical manuals) that temporal realities, as well as those of the spiritual world, possess a definite value in themselves — as we should have known from our Scriptures and which the humane author of *Mater et Magistra* and *Pacem in Terris* recalled for us. (How different the approach here from the famous denial in the 1864 *Syllabus* that "the Roman Pontiff can and ought to reconcile himself and reach agreement with progress, liberalism and modern civilization"!) In the *Church in the Modern World* (the longest document of Vatican II), written "to the whole of humanity," examining "how it conceives of the presence and activity of the Church in the world today" (art. 2), there is an obvious effort to view what is positive in the movements of the Secular City: its intellectual climate, forms of culture, its advances in the historical, social, and psychological sciences — with a more personalist approach to those political and economic principles laid down in previous papal encyclicals. A striking note of the Constitution is the conscious attempt of the Church to place herself at the service of man as he is today, seeking "to speak to all men in order to shed light on the mystery of man and to co-operate in finding a solution to the outstanding problems of our times" (art. 10). This attitude may not have found favor with certain Lutheran theologians for whom the world (and the Church) are seen to be under judgment before the uncompromising challenge of the Gospel. But coopera-tion need not mean accommodation to the world's standards, even less capitulation.

Within this background of openness to what the world has to offer, we have to try to list some of the more im-portant contributions which are making an impact on Catho-lic scholars and which will merit more serious attention in future textbooks than a summary relegation to *errores*.

PHILOSOPHY

In the first place there are the worthy gleanings from modern philosophies. Whatever invective our teachers have been accustomed to hurl at any not fathered by Aristotle and baptized by Aquinas, it is now recognized that contemporary philosophies do offer in some measure a conceptual framework for communicating the message of salvation to those of our time. In those early days when the Church was young, Platonism was largely in vogue to communicate that message. When the Arab philosophers, Averroes and Avicenna, resurrected Aristotle, St. Thomas showed how this *revenant* could also subserve Christian theology. And today St. Thomas himself should be one, but only one, of the sources of philosophical investigation. It is simply unrealistic to neglect — in the supposed interests of orthodox Catholicism (a mistake Rahner has never made) — Kierkegaard, Heidegger, Wittgenstein. Uncritical panegyrists of mediaeval scholasticism fail to recognize its limitations, assuming a once-for-all sufficiency.

There are many gospel truths which modern thought has brought with some consequence to our errant outlook — a greater appreciation of the human person, his freedom, responsibility, conscience, all of which received new emphasis in the Council. Many more insights could be mentioned, but perhaps that aspect which has been most influential in the orientation of Catholic theological studies has been the application of existentialist categories to certain questions. It would be impossible here to even outline the various types of existentialist philosophers who have made their mark, or the various forms their expositions (largely in the form of current literature: journals, novels, plays, etc.) have taken. Perhaps it might be sufficient to say that there is an overall preoccupation with man, the individual, in his concrete situation where, amidst suffering, frustration, the apparent meaninglessness of life, he has to find his "self" by his personal and responsible choosing despite surrounding anxious insecurity. The Medieval Schoolmen may have said *agere sequitur esse;* but now it is *esse sequitur agere:* a man is what he does. (It is not hard to see how the controversial "situation ethics," where the morality of an act derived from its concrete circumstances, was a foreseeable result of existentialism.) Continental Lutheran and Reform theologians, painfully aware of the anguish and disillusionment of millions after the upheavals of two world wars, found a ready audience with their demand for a blind leap of faith in Christ, whose story challenges modern man to a decision to join himself to a crucified and risen Christ so that man, too, may win a new existence, a new understanding of self. And in a system of thought where people are more important than things (was there not at least latent in scholasticism a tendency to consider an individual somewhat after the nature of a static essence?), there is an emphasis on person-to-person relationships, an "I-You" rather than an "I-It" approach. When we come to look at the revitalized notions of, e.g., revelation and the sacraments, we shall see that valuable perspectives have been opened for us.

THE SCIENCES OF MAN

The second sphere of modern activity where our theology has been able to collect useful data is in the sciences of man: psychology, anthropology, sociology. It should be needless to recall how the "psychology" of our seminary manuals left us completely unprepared for the startling advances our companions were assimilating in other centers, even if sometimes Jungian archetypes and Freudian symbols monopolized the attention deeper studies deserved. The complex layers that go to make up a personality are being investigated and some light is already being thrown on moral behavior patterns and the psychological influences at work in faith and witness. In the depths of a person, grace is interwoven with nature.

And then, face to face with scientific gains in anthropology, questions are being asked anew about man's emergence, the problem of hominization, of original sin, of man's continuing evolution toward a total perfection. The literature on Teilhard de Chardin shows signs of becoming a shoreless sea. Criticisms of his writings as being a goulash of poetry, mysticism, theology, and science have failed to diminish the interest occasioned by the problems he posed rather than by the answers he gave. Here was a Catholic who was echoing the sounds from secular anvils. A "Christian Anthropology" will have to be a necessary tract in our manuals of the future, complementing — if not replacing — the meager treatment of "Adam."

SECULAR THEOLOGY

Finally, to complete our conspectus of forces at work in the "other dialogue," we have to look at the Church confronting modern secularization. The Anglican Bishop of Woolwich, John A. T. Robinson, in his *Honest to God* and *The New Reformation?*, popularized for English and American readers three German theologians who seemed to speak of God with a new and incisive relevance: Paul Tillich, with his *Shaking of the Foundations*, Dietrich Bonhoeffer with his *Letters and Papers from Prison*, and Rudolf Bultmann with his *New Testament and Mythology*. The Bishop articulated problems that plagued the minds of many: (1) The traditional presentation of God that lies behind most minds as someone at hand in necessity, an escape hatch from the difficulties of life, or in our progressive, technological age which can explain and resolve so many past obscurities, an irrelevancy. (2) The language and thought-forms employed to communicate the Christian message — are they not meaningless in this day and age to so many? (3) How far do the time-honored institutions of organized religion carry any weight with a post-Christian society that is highly industrialized, technological? Robinson's writings evoked controversy in the English-speaking world (his 1967 follow-up,

Exploration into God, is not the same pacesetter), and similar discussions have been taking place over the works of "secular" theologians like Harvey Cox and the much more radical essays of the "death of God" theologians, William Hamilton, Thomas Altizer, and Paul Van Buren. The answer of the Anglican theologian, E. L. Mascall, that such theologians have capitulated to our secular environment does nothing to relieve the tension that their descriptions make so vivid. The serious situation they present must call for consideration from theologians as to how and in what measure the Christian message and witness can recapture the ground that has so extensively been lost. *The Church in the Modern World* has no hesitation in laying some blame for atheism on believers themselves (art. 19), on the distance that separates the Gospel and its messengers (art. 43). The English Downside Symposium of 1964, *Theology and the University*, has suggested that theological reflection, to be effective, cannot ignore the personal, temporal, and historical aspects of human existence. Contact with secular disciplines, secular culture, secular advances in so many fields, we have seen, is the plea of the Constitution. It has been the contribution of the authors we have mentioned that some important thoroughfares in *The Secular City* have been indexed. We shall refer to them in more detail later.

Suggestions for further reading

John MacQuarrie, *Twentieth-Century Religious Thought* (New York: Harper and Row, 1963); *Theology and the University*, ed. J. Coulson (Baltimore: Helicon, 1964); *Twentieth Century Thinkers*, ed. J. K. Ryan (Staten Island: Alba House, 1965); G. Jansen, *An Existentialist Approach to Theology* (Milwaukee: Bruce, 1966); B. Wicker, *Toward a Contemporary Christianity* (Notre Dame, Ind.: University of Notre Dame, 1967); R. Adolfs, *The Grave of God* (New York: Harper & Row, 1967); G. Hibbert, *Man, Culture and Christianity* (London: Sheed & Ward, 1967).

2. The Forces at Work From the Churches

GROWING ECUMENISM

The recent film, *Fahrenheit 451*, with its pyromaniac destruction of books, may suggest to many a ready solution for the types of reading material now available at counters where previously solid Catholic literature was the only need envisaged, or supplied. Today, learned German faces stare uncomprehendingly at parochial pictorials, Protestant paperbacks beckon from the revolving cases, and Rahner and Ramsey stand unrepentantly with Ripley. The offense is compounded with joint services: common prayers said, common hymns sung, a mini-theology preached that covers the beliefs of most denominations. Converts to Catholicism wonder, was it worth while when, for them, things seem to be returning to the *status quo ante.* Luther has been reinstated, Tübingen replaced on Catholic maps, and you can now make your annual retreat at Taizé. Inquire why earlier coexistence among the churches has become cooperation and you will be told that we have become "ecumenical."

In the previous chapter we had a look at the first of three dialogues in which the present Church is involved and which future theology cannot afford to neglect: the dialogue with

9

the world, which lay behind the pastoral Constitution *The Church in the Modern World*. We have now to see something of the dialogue between the Christian churches (in the light of the decree on Ecumenism) and of the dialogue within the Catholic Church among her theologians.

The January Unity Octave has been well established among Catholics as a means of promoting a return to the fold of other Christian bodies. A more organized ecumenical movement, however, has existed among those Christian churches for some fifty years: there is the World Council of Churches and a growth in the groupings and merging of non-Catholic sects. Catholics are now becoming more open to such movements. On January 25, 1959, Pope John stated his intention of calling an ecumenical council, "not only for the spiritual good and joy of the Christian people," but also "to invite the separated communities to seek again that unity for which so many souls are longing in these days throughout the world." In the Council itself observers were present from other Christian communities and a Secretariat for Christian Unity, with the status of a Council Commission, was erected. During the Council discussions a concern could be noticed not to alienate unnecessarily members of other Christian communities.

After many reworkings on the drafts on "Ecumenism," the final decree laid emphasis on the notion of a pilgrim Church moving amid difficulties toward Christ rather than on a movement of "return" of Christian bodies to the Roman Church. Besides recognition of their truly Christian endowments, it was acknowledged that the work of God's grace could result in "a more ample realization of the very mystery of Christ and the Church" (art. 4). Jesus in his Spirit is at work in the churches and communities beyond the visible borders of the Catholic Church. Believers in Christ, who are truly baptized are truly reborn, are our brothers, and God uses their worship to sanctify and save them. There was also the admission that divisions among Christians are the result of sin on both sides (art. 1, 3), with a plea for common repentance and mutual forgiveness (art. 7). The obligation was stressed, too, for all Christians to work and pray for unity, without, however, any "false conciliatory approach" (art. 11) in matters of doctrine. The reference to Catholic and Protestant thinking about "the relationship between the Scriptures and the Church" (art. 21), while indicating one such difference in doctrine, is to be seen, nevertheless, at the side of an emphasis on Scripture in the Catholic Church which helps reduce that difference. There is further the decision that "in special certain circumstances" it is "allowable, indeed desirable" that Catholics "join in prayer with their separated brethren" (art. 8) — a decision that was put into action with Paul VI joining with Protestant and Orthodox observers at a unity service during the last week of the Council in Rome itself. We are becoming accustomed, also, to meetings between Catholic and non-Catholic theologians. Finally, "cooperation among all Christians" is commended, with the suggestion that it be "increasingly developed" in the task of improving modern conditions (art. 21).

This decree, so different from the cautionary encyclical *Mortalium Animos* of 1928, the Holy Office *Monitum* of June 5, 1948, and the *Instructio* of December 20, 1949 (not to mention certain sections of the Code of Canon Law), received favorable attention from non-Catholic theologians. "This is more than the opening of a door; new ground has been broken. No Catholic document has ever spoken of non-Catholic Christians in this way" (Dr. Oscar Cullmann). Yet, some reserve was felt with the Decree's statement that the Catholic Church is the only true Church (art. 3), with papal primacy and jurisdiction over the whole Church. From the Catholic side, there have been warnings not to overstep due limits in doctrinal and liturgical differences in (what has been called) an "ecumania." Courtesy and candor should be the twin controls directing all communication between us.

BARTH, BRUNNER, BULTMANN,
AND CULLMANN

With the Decree on Ecumenism in mind, let us examine in outline the contributions which non-Catholic theologians have been able to offer present Catholic theology. It is evidently impossible to sound a roll call of influential names and works but certain dominant trends may be noted. For the purposes of clarity we may distinguish three main ones: the "encounter theology," associated principally with the names of Karl Barth and Emil Brunner; the "existentialist theology" of Rudolf Bultmann and his school; and the "salvation-history theology" of Oscar Cullmann. It should not be necessary to point out that on a variety of themes these theologians show a measure of agreement while remaining largely at variance with each other.

The view of Protestants of the Lutheran and Reformed traditions that the Bible is not to be read as a catalog of propositions listed for our acceptance and belief, but rather as the account of man's meeting with God, has found wide acceptance among Catholic scholars who, for too long, have used the Bible as a static statement of truths serving as a basis for theologizing. This encounter, we are told, is not confined to the past events recorded in the sacred writings: God is still meeting and challenging man, and the Bible gives us the unchanging pattern of God's intervention in the affairs of man, in the life of the individual. Further, utterly sinful human nature can do nothing of itself to merit this grace of God given us in Christ. Total humanity is under the judgment of God, and justification can be achieved only through faith in Christ. It was Barth's genius to recall these principles to a world of liberal Protestantism in which (to quote Reinhold Niebuhr) "A God without wrath brought men without sin into a kingdom without judgment through the ministrations of a Christ without a cross."

Now, while Emil Brunner will admit a revelation in creation (the "Natural Theology" of our textbooks) which needed the Christ-Event to give it its true meaning and orientation, and will admit, too, a present possibility for every man to share in that encounter of God and man in Christ, Karl Barth, thoroughly skeptical of man's naked attempt to contemplate God even on a natural level, will not grant even that vague groping allowed by Brunner. For Barth, the only theology is to be found in God's appropriating of human thought to his revelation in Christ. God, and God alone, will provide the "point of contact" between revelation and human thought. A philosophy may be used to make articulate the encounter between God and man, but its demonstrative value is precisely nil. Theology must derive from revelation, not from human speculation, and this theology must transform the student by confronting him with God's challenge, rather than by indoctrinating him. Theology, then (and preaching), does not begin with abstract ideas which are, in Barth's words, nothing but "a piece of paper, a great noise, only ideas," but with the reality engraven in the kerygma of God's encounter with man with its challenge and response, its faith, commitment, and living witness.

Rudolf Bultmann, on the other hand, will isolate the significance of the events of Christ's life, death, and resurrection from the facts themselves, and will see these facts as nothing more than the symbols, the vehicles for Christ's message. The facts have no importance besides the truth conveyed. In any case, Bultmann continues, we know nothing of the actual words and deeds of Jesus since they have been passed on to us as creative interpretations of the primitive Church around the figure of Jesus. Lastly, Bultmann attempts to demythologize the language and content of the New Testament, to free it from the shackles of an ancient thought-form meaningless to modern man.

Oscar Cullman, finally, in oposition to Bultmann, insists on the historical nature of the accounts which go to make up the kerygma. This, for the Old and New Testaments, is "salvation-history," i.e., both saving history and the history of salvation. God acts in history and within this action of God we can trace a plan which opens with Adam and the whole human race, begins to narrow with Abraham and the Hebrews, then with the Israelites down to the pious Jews (such as the figures in our Infancy Narratives of Matthew and Luke), with the climax in Christ himself. The plan now broadens out: Christ, the apostles and disciples, the Church, and lastly the whole of mankind and creation. As to theology, Cullman (e.g., in his *Christology of the New Testament*) says that this must not be expressed in terms derived from Greek philosophy but in biblical terms, in terms of "event." Thus his christology is "functional" rather than essentialist — Christ's titles give us a framework for considering his saving acts, rather than questions of "nature," "person," "hypostatic union," etc.

To summarize the contribution of non-Catholic scholars to present Catholic theology, we might describe it thus: we have been called to a greater appreciation of how the Word of God in the Scriptures with its dynamism and might acts in the history of salvation. We have been forced to acknowledge the influence of the primitive Church in transmitting and forming our Gospels, even if we cannot (with Bultmann) deny the validity of the historical facts underlying the Christian message nor see in the kerygma a pure creation of the Church. Lastly, Bultmann's program of demythologizing has emphasized the need of communicating the Gospel message in a form that is meaningful to men of our time.

If it might seem that the contribution of Anglican and Free Church theology has been unfairly excluded, it has to be recognized that it is on the continent that the impact of non-Catholic theologians has been most acutely felt in modern Catholic theology, and this from the Lutheran and Reform traditions. On the other hand, one cannot ignore the pivotal studies of such writers as C. H. Dodd, Gregory Dix, L. S. Thornton, D. M. Baillie, A. M. Hunter, E. L.

Mascall . . . with their investigations in the fields of biblical and philosophical theology.

CATHOLIC PACESETTERS

As to the dialogue among theologians inside the Church, we have only to glance at the annotated edition by Walter M. Abbot of *The Documents of Vatican II* to see the forces at work, and their result: a deeper appreciation of the mystery of the Church, of revelation, the liturgy, the role of bishops, priests, deacons, religious, the laity — the list is endless. Practical consequences have been felt particularly in liturgical renewal, with its introduction of the vernacular, concelebration, the emphasis on the proclamation of the Word, group "confession," biblical vigils, the view of the sacraments as a meeting with Christ.

The Catholic theologians concerned with these advances are now household gods (or swearwords) among many for whom Hervé, Tanquery, Noldin, and Génicot with their standard textbooks would have been unknown and ignored. After the early semiscientific work of Karl Adam and Romano Guardini in Germany, we have had the outspoken popularizations of Hans Küng (retelling and applying to the Council period his previous scientific work). Karl Rahner, difficult to read in German or English, then entered the mesmerized Anglo-Saxon world with his theology on nature and grace, Church and sacrament, the world, the "anonymous Christian" in works which were probes rather than conclusions. A younger generation of German theologians are taking up his questions and are investigating the problems he has posed. Bernhard Häring, Hofinger, and Jungmann need no comment.

Lest anything non-German be considered not germane to theology, we have to note the work of the Dutch theologian, E. H. Schillebeeckx, on the sacraments as encounter with Christ and his three-volume survey on marriage which has appeared in English. Louvain theologians have not been idle; Gustav Thils' notion of a "theology of terrestrial realities" should prevent our philosophy and theology from remaining (to use the words of Archbishop Hurley of Durban) "like the sediment on the bed of a canal rarely sufficiently disturbed to mix with the flowing waters of mental experience and reaction"; we have to learn "how to re-enter the world of movement." In France, besides the work of biblical specialists, we have seen the reinstatement of De Lubac and Daniélou with their studies in patristics, early Christianity, and typology. Yves Congar wrote early and well on disunited Christianity, and his later works on reform in the Church, on a theology of the laity, and on poverty played their part in conciliar thought. I have already referred to Teilhard de Chardin, that most controversial figure.

Yet the center of development for Catholic theological thought seems to be shifting from the old world to the new. Fr. Schillebeeckx and the French Jesuit, Henri Rondet, have remarked that Americans will be the trailblazers for the theology of the future. American theologians, both lay and clerical, are no longer simply offshoots of European schools. Laymen like Novak, Callahan, Dewart, clerics like the late John Courtney Murray, John L. McKenzie, Gabriel Moran, start from a different base. Much of their theology owes a lot to the American scene.

In following chapters, I hope to show more specifically how such cross-fertilization from secular, non-Catholic, and Catholic thought must effect the various treatises that have made up our courses in theology.

Suggestions for further reading

Christianity Divided, ed. D. J. Callahan, et al. (New York: Sheed & Ward, 1961); *The New Theologians*, ed. R. R. Acheson (London: Mowbrays, 1964); *Steps to Christian Unity*, ed. J. A. O'Brien (New York: Doubleday, 1964); G. C. Berkouwer, *The Second Vatican Council and the New Catholicism* (Grand Rapids: Eerdmans, 1965); *Ecumenical Experiences*, ed. Luis V. Romeu (Westminster, Md.: Newman, 1965).

3. The Word of God Transmitted in the Church

The past-century Tübingen Catholic theologian, John Adam Möhler, gave us the dictum that Church, Gospel, and Tradition will always stand or fall together. The four-act drama that was played out around the Constitution on Divine Revelation amply emphasizes the importance of this fact. The preliminary draft entitled De Fontibus Revelationis — a reprint, really, of so much of our earlier textbook treatment on revelation where the treatise was drawn up as a force de frappe against pagans, rationalists, and (of course) Protestants — was returned because it failed to pay sufficient attention to a proclamation of Christian truth in all its living and challenging reality to men of our time.

It was a mere warhead of apologetics at a time when various issues dealt with in fundamental theology were beginning to be viewed from the standpoint of their theological content rather than from their previous status as defense-mechanisms of the Church against outside invasions. Further, this first draft took for granted (as shown by its very title) that there are two independent and parallel sources of revelation in the sense that revelation is partly contained in Scripture and partly in Tradition, so that we may expect to find

17

doctrines supplied by Tradition which are not contained in
Scripture. It had been proposed that this view was that of
the Council of Trent but recent re-examination of that
Council's proceedings has called this into question.

After the rejection of the preliminary draft on the intervention of Pope John in November, 1962, a second draft,
largely rewritten and more biblical in cast and content, was
prepared for the second session of 1963. This was put to
the vote in the third session of 1964 when a number of
amendments were proposed. On November 18, 1965, after
a series of last-minute corrections from Pope Paul, the Constitution was finally promulgated. The pronouncement of
Vatican II on the Bible, *Divine Revelation*, is one of the
most pivotal documents emerging from the Council since
it deals specifically with God's word to man, upon which
all the teaching of the Council must ultimately depend.

No mere theological treatise, it is designed as a proclamation: "This most sacred Synod takes its direction from these
words of St. John: 'We announce to you the eternal life
which was with the Father, and has appeared to us'" (art. 1).

The first chapter describes revelation itself as event and
interpretation (art. 2), beginning in creation (art. 3, 6)
with its climax in the revelation of Christ (art. 3, 4). The
second chapter continues to place the Bible within the framework of the whole of Christian doctrine on salvation by
dealing now with the transmission of revelation. The nature
and function of Scripture and Tradition are broached (art.
7, 8, 9) as also that of the *magisterium* (art. 10), which is
to serve the Word of God. The role of the faithful in the
transmission and development of doctrine is expressed in
terms which Luke applied to Mary who "kept all these things
in her heart, pondering them" (art. 8). Chapter three opens
with the more specific treatment of sacred Scripture, taking
up the questions of divine inspiration and the interpretation
of Scripture.

As to the thorny problem of biblical inerrancy, the Constitution states that "the books of Scripture must be acknowl-

edged as teaching firmly, faithfully, and without error that truth which God wanted put into the sacred writings *for the sake of our salvation*" (art. 11). This phrase, a last-minute change, was substituted for the words "tending to salvation" (*salutaris*) which had qualified the word "truth." The change was made lest "tending to salvation" would seem to limit the extent of the truth itself to those things only which dealt precisely with salvation. Yet, as R. A. F. MacKenzie has shown, the point made is essentially the same:

> The Bible was not written in order to teach the natural sciences, nor to give information on merely political history. It treats of these (and all other subjects) only insofar as they are involved in matters concerning salvation. It is only in this respect that the veracity of God and the inerrancy of the inspired writers are engaged. This is not a quantitative distinction, as though some sections treated of salvation (and were inerrant), while others gave merely natural knowledge (and were fallible). It is formal, and applies to the whole text. The latter is authoritative and inerrant in what it affirms about the revelation of God and the history of salvation. According to the intentions of its authors, divine and human, it makes no other affirmations (*The Documents of Vatican II*, ed. Walter M. Abbott, S.J., p. 119, n. 31).

Literary forms employed in the Bible are to be examined "if we are to search out the intention of the sacred writers" (art. 12). The same article tells how Scripture is its own best commentary, with Scripture scholars helping the Church's understanding of it to mature.

With chapter four we have an outline of salvation history in the Old Testament, with its climax in Christ recorded for us in the New. Chapter five deals principally with the Gospels which have "a special pre-eminence . . . for they are the principal witness of the life and teaching of the incarnate Word, our Savior" (art. 18). These, despite their complex origin and formation, tell us "the honest truth about Jesus" (art. 19). A sixth and final chapter is concerned with the Bible in the life of the Church: "easy access to sacred Scripture should be provided for all the Christian

faithful" (art. 22), with students and clergy, deacons and
catechists encouraged to diligent sacred reading and careful
study for their ministry of the word. Finally, the Council
hoped for "a new surge of spiritual vitality from intensified
veneration for God's word, which 'lasts forever' " (art. 26).

There are doubtless many points one should like to have
seen developed in the Constitution. We might have expected a more detailed analysis of the relationship between
Scripture and Tradition, although (it must be admitted)
the investigations of theologians are not yet sufficiently ripe
for a hard and fast solution. The question, too, of inerrancy
needs a wider treatment particularly with regard to historical
writing in the Old Testament. For the Gospels the Constitution was satisfied largely with summarizing much of the
Instruction of 1964 which was aimed at protecting the his-
toricity of the infancy and resurrection narratives. There are
immense problems involved in the formation of the Gospels
and it is often difficult to determine the quantity of cold
fact behind these interpretative records.

ENCOUNTER AND TRANSMISSION

If we try to isolate the theological thought that lies behind the Constitution we shall find that there is an inter-
play between salvation history and encounter theology. One
may also notice the beginning of what might be called a
"theology of tradition." A word is called for on these points.

When we open the Bible, we cannot ignore how revelation
is constantly tied up with the human situation, with history.
God's revelation took place within the specific history of
a definite race group, Israel, in a graph which was described
on the events of Israel's developing life. The calling of Abraham, the liberation of the Exodus, the conquest of Canaan,
the establishment of the Israelite nation with its theocratic
monarchy, the continual subjugation under foreign powers,
the catastrophe of the deportations to Babylon, the restoration — all these events were interpreted within the perspec-

tives of God's designs. God was meeting man, not only in the rarefied atmosphere of thought but in the tremendous, inescapable facts of his daily life. Revelation was formidably real. On a more personal basis the prophets and the humanists of the wisdom movement had a more intimate message for the individual also.

The New Testament carries on the same process, but now in Christ God meets individuals as a man among men and the climax of revelation is found in circumstances of the most palpable domesticity. And it is the burden of the New Testament writings that the exalted Lord now lives and is still present to the community of believers. The deists of the seventeenth century (a century generally deficient in a sense of history) could claim that revelation was superfluous since God could be known by the "light of reason." But while this is so, it is only in history that a *personal* God could be revealed unambiguously. The forces released at Cape Kennedy, like the forces of nature, do not reveal a person with whom one may have personal relationship.

Within an historical context, revelation was the manifestation by God — first of all of himself, and secondarily of his will and intentions. What God revealed was not a series of propositions to be believed but a person to be met. Hence the importance attached to salvation history and encounter theology which is such a feature of modern theological writing. An outstanding example of this is *A New Catechism* (the "Dutch Catechism") where the salvation history approach is seen in the very plan of the book: Part I poses the question of the mystery of man's existence; Part II places this human situation within the background of human attempts to find an answer in Hinduism, Buddhism, and Islam, with the beginning of a solution in Israel; Part III gives the answer in Christ; Part IV continues the history of salvation in the apostolic and post-apostolic Church, and in the present daily life of the Christian with his experience of sin and grace, prayer and the sacraments; the final consummation of all things is treated in Part V, and it is only here, after

seeing the action of God throughout history, that his attributes can be examined. This salvation history approach
has the remarkable advantage of linking Christian truth with
Christian living, a healthy existentialism far removed from
the cold, static essentialism of our textbooks, where things
were more important than living persons.

Now this revelation of God, his self-giving to man, is of
its nature destined for the good of all men; it is of itself
public. Transmitted orally it becomes tradition; recorded in
writing it becomes sacred Scripture. The Scriptures, then,
contain all revelation in their written record, but not all
that is in Scripture — and this is a significant point — is
revelation. The encounter between God and man, taking
place within well-defined historical circumstances, lends to
the description of such an encounter a kaleidoscopic variety.
Not only are we seeing revelation given; we are also seeing
the response of man to it. In the Old Testament as well
as in the New, much that is found is the record of the
effects of revelation on its recipients, of human reactions to
it. But it is often difficult to show by chapter and verse
where one may uncover a formal revelation as distinct (for
example, in the Gospels) from the theological reflection on
such a revelation. All Scripture is inspired, but not all of
it is revelation.

Similarly for Tradition, this includes much that is of
purely human origin — the response of man, ancient but
man-made traditions alongside the transmitted revelation of
Christ. One should have to distinguish the Tradition of the
Church, continuing the oral preaching of the Apostles, making explicit the pattern of God's dealings with men for each
day and age — from traditions in the Church which derive
from man alone. Oral transmission of God's revelation enshrined, and is enshrined by, the splendor of the written
Word.

It is through the living magisterium that constant and
renewed interpretation and application to new situations of
the message of the Scriptures is effected. No mere human

instrument, it operates under the guidance of that Spirit who teaches all things, bringing back to errant minds all that Christ had said and done. Yet this charismatic influence of the Spirit is not confined to the *ecclesia docens;* the faithful, too, have their role to play in pondering over, in living, in bringing to maturity the message of Christ. Tradition is no collection of fossilized statements nor an imposing line of the Fathers of the Church. It is rather the Word of God living in the Church, working through all her members. It is constantly developing and has constantly to be rethought in the light of the total movement of human life.

The meeting of God and man still continues, and this personal encounter is now effected in and through the Word which he has addressed to us in Christ. The pattern of revelation as found in the Scriptures of event and word, of divine intervention and explanation, is maintained in the Church through her sacraments and her proclamation of the word. Here, that meeting is found in its most compelling form. And the Church herself is the sacrament of God's self-revelation to the whole world, the abiding sign of his presence among all men, calling all to salvation.

Suggestions for further reading

G. Moran, *Scripture and Tradition* (New York: Herder and Herder, 1963); ——— *Theology of Revelation* (New York: Herder and Herder, 1965); J. L. McKenzie, *The Power and the Wisdom* (Milwaukee: Bruce, 1965).

4. God in a World Come of Age

Not too long ago the American Methodist student magazine, *Motive*, ran the following obituary:

> ATLANTA, Ga., Nov. 9. — God, creator of the universe, principal deity of the world's Jews, ultimate reality of Christians, and most eminent of all divinities, died late yesterday during major surgery undertaken to correct a massive diminishing influence. Reaction from the world's great and from the man in the street was uniformly incredulous . . .

This satire was directed at the new theology without a *theos* emerging in the United States from the so-called "death of God" theologians — principally William Hamilton (*The New Essence of Christianity*), Thomas Altizer (*The Gospel of Christian Atheism*), and Paul Van Buren (*The Secular Meaning of the Gospel*). According to them, man is now living in an era that has seen God become the helpless amputee of history; his death an event (Altizer tells us) datable in our own lifetime. For Van Buren, even the word "God" is dead. What remains for these theologians is the man Jesus with the meaning of his life and death, his values and perspectives readily available to all.

To understand something of the converging factors which

24

have led to such a nontheology we have to trace our steps
back to the classical, traditional teaching and observe how,
with the increasing control man is acquiring of his environment, older postulates for the existence of a monitoring deity
have lost much of their urgency.

Vatican II, in its Constitution on Revelation, recalled
much that Vatican I had taught on how God may be known
from reason alone. Similarly, the Declaration on Non-Christian Religions states that "From ancient times down to the
present, there has existed among diverse peoples a certain
perception of that hidden power which hovers over the course
of things and over the events of human life; at times, indeed,
recognition can be found of a supreme Divinity and of a
Supreme Father too" (art. 2). In the same article Hinduism
and Buddhism are specifically mentioned. God revealed something of himself in nature, and the various religions of an-
tiquity represent genuine efforts to come to grips with the
powerful forces mysteriously enshrined in nature and which
are in some way a natural revelation of the power of God
himself. We are accustomed to think of St. Thomas' "five
proofs" as demonstrating the existence of God, yet primitive
efforts to deify the mysteries of nature — death, birth, fer-
tility, love, light, etc. — were attempts to teach that Something which was felt to be behind these phenomena. But a
sin-marred humanity could only arrive at grotesque and
mutilated theologies. Even the traces of God's law in man's
conscience were confused in the chaos caused by sin. Wick-
edness, Paul reminds us in Romans, suppressed the truth.

But God decided to cut the knot of sin and myth by
entering history and the climax of his self-revelation was in
Christ. Now men would be able to see clearly how very
personal was the divinity which governed their lives. While
"natural theology" insists that in theory God can be demon-
strated from pure reason, in the concrete God has given his
enlightening grace to all men to lead them to faith and
love. Among the unevangelized such a knowledge may be
implicit and obscure, but this awareness is no purely natural

knowledge. Because grace is involved there is some experience of faith. God's Word was at work among all peoples, at all times, and in all places. God is not the exclusive property of the Church but is acting in history as he wills, meeting man in the most unlikely situations.

Yet the revelation of God in nature and in history is increasingly becoming irrelevant to modern man. Nietzsche's thesis that striving, self-centered man has killed God is not quite the naïve assumption condemned in our textbooks. The Danish philosopher, Søren Kierkegaard, predicted in the past century that a time was coming when man would not feel the same need for God and for religion as did the earlier centuries of Christianity. In our own time Dietrich Bonhoeffer could envisage from his concentration camp a "religionless Christianity" in a "world come of age" through man's mastery of his destiny and his rejection of institutionalized forms of religion which were bound up with dated thought patterns and emotional needs no longer experienced.

And then there have been so many misconceptions of what God is — from the ludicrous image resembling (Frank Sheed muses in his Theology and Sanity) Karl Marx or Lord Tennyson, to a Great Unknown, "up there" above us, "out there" beyond us, referred to in time of need or to explain the anomalies of everyday life. Small wonder, then, that Karl Rahner could tell his students in Innsbruck, "Your God is dead"; understandable, too, that the Lutheran theologian, Paul Tillich, could advise, "You must forget everything traditional you have learned about God, perhaps even that word itself." The linguistic philosopher, Anthony Flew, finds that God is being "killed by inches," dying "the death of a thousand qualifications" as man learns more and more to dispense with God in explaining his environment, the forces at work in his life. Add to this the atheism of distraction: people are just too busy to worry about God at all, as Fr. Courtney Murray has described it. John Robinson, the Anglican Bishop of Woolwich, has summarized the three thrusts of modern atheism thus: (1) God is intellectually superfluous

— man has learned to cope with questions of importance without recourse to God as a working hypothesis; (2) God is emotionally dispensable — man is discovering how to stop treating God as a peg, a refuge, a compensation for the miseries he should be fighting; (3) God is morally intolerable — a God who "causes" or "allows" the suffering of a single child cannot be permitted.

SECULARIZATION

The one constant factor that has been dominant in modern life is secularization: the historical process wherein man increasingly controls the universe, principally through his advances in science and technology. Nature is no longer sacred; science can pursue its course of investigating the intelligibility of the universe without recourse to God for the explanation of mysterious causes still undefined. Technology does not hesitate, consequently, to intrude into practical experiments with people and things formerly considered "sacred." An urbanized city culture is established, industrialized and far removed from the idyllic, rural temperament of earlier times and not yet able to construct symbols (as did the past) to help us understand God. In *The Secular City* Harvey Cox defines secularization as "the loosing of the world from religious and quasi-religious understandings of itself, the dispelling of all closed world views, the breaking of all supernatural myths and sacred symbols"; men do not need to postulate God to explain, administer, or justify certain areas of life.

Hand in hand with secularization has gone dechristianization, a general diminishing of Christian faith. Now, while these two processes have developed together historically, are interrelated, manifest similar causes, yet — and this is important — they are distinguishable. Indeed, because secularization is not yet "secularism" (agnostic humanism, which excludes all possibility of something beyond this world, declaring this world to be all there is), it can challenge Chris-

tians "to purify their concept of the sacred and achieve a
unity of secular and sacred which does not confuse but
clearly differentiates them" (Charles Davis, God's Grace in
History, p. 20).

One who has profoundly dealt with this problem of the
apparent threat from secularization to Christianity is the
German Lutheran theologian, Friederich Gogarten. He believes that man's increasing dominion over the world is a
divine gift to man that is rooted in biblical revelation. He
sees in secularization two distinct but related trends. There
is the rejection of organized forms of religion which were
tied to aspects of culture now past: art, politics, education,
even economics were seen as the proper sphere of the Church,
subject to the immediate intervention of God. God was
made part of that culture and when that culture underwent
changes, belief in the action of God linked to such a culture
changed. And then, as has already been remarked, man was
becoming master of his own fate, now accepting the responsibility he had previously delegated to God. (The Dutch
Dominican, Eduard Schillebeeckx, has said, "God has dis-
appeared because of the image of him that the Church used
for many, many ages.")

Gogarten points out that secularization has its root in
the message of the Old and New Testaments: instead of
a narrow, cribbed-in view of life, man's freedom under God
in the world is proclaimed. St. Paul, to protect the Galatians
from the hodge-podge of Judaizing superstition and Gnostic
extravaganza which could jeopardize the liberty they had
acquired in Christ, wrote, "During our minority we were
slaves to the elemental spirits of the universe, but . . . God
sent his own Son . . . to purchase freedom for the subjects
of the law" (Gal 4:3–4, NEB). Gogarten goes on to say
that secularization should be considered as a consequence
of Christ's teaching men to take responsibility for life in
all its phases. Dr. J. B. Metz, a student of Rahner, has
described secularization as being "in its origin a Christian
event." This implies an openness to both the transcendent

mystery of being and the yet undiscovered possibilities of
the future. Thus is man, in his own situation as creature,
open to encounter with God. God is no forgotten creator
of a distant past but a hidden God who seeks man among
the earthly realities with which he lives, to which he is tied.
Karl Rahner (*The Christian in the Market-place*, pp. 118–
119) sees the present apparent eclipse of God as a sign only
that the world is experiencing his "anonymous presence":

> The secular world, as secular, has an inner mysterious depth,
> in all its earthly mysteries from birth to death, through which,
> by the grace of God, it is open to God and his infinitely in-
> comprehensible love even when it is not, before receiving
> the explicit message of the gospel, aware of it. Not only are
> there many anonymous Christians; there is also an anony-
> mously Christian world. For whenever its demands and its
> reality are really met and endured in the whole breadth and
> depth of natural human existence and in the totality of a
> human life, then, according to Christian teaching, the grace
> of Christ is already at work and this response and endurance
> are already something Christian, though they may be ex-
> plicitly only secular and natural.

Moreover God, the "ground of being" (Tillich), can show
himself in what Bishop Ian Ramsey has called "discernment
situations" — times of crisis for the individual or the community where man is thrust back from so much of the
artificiality that makes up life to consider anew the deeper
implications of his existence, his area of ultimate concern.

THE SPIRIT OF GOD

This hidden power and presence of God in the world
and among humanity is nothing less than a continuing incarnation of all things into Christ who now works through
his Spirit. It may not be too much to suggest that in some
way this Holy Spirit is finding at last the place that should
be his among Christians. The 1964 meeting of the World
Alliance of Reformed and Presbyterian Churches in Frank-
furt chose as its theme "Come Creator Spirit"; a similar

theme was discussed in the first ecumenical meeting in
Chicago of Catholics and Methodists; for 1968 the World
Council of Churches has as its topic God's promise of renewal to mankind through the Spirit: "Behold, I make all
things new." Among Catholics, Vatican II brought a greater
realization of the charismatic role of the Spirit acting throughout the whole Church — hierarchy and laity — for the development of doctrine and the revitalization of Christian life.

Further, many, taken up with the escalating involvement
of the churches in the secular world, would perceive an intensified outpouring of God's sanctifying Spirit beyond the
boundaries of those churches and ecclesial communities.
Movements for social justice, world peace, the alleviation of
misery and hunger — all these and many more manifest the
working of the Spirit of God who can speak to the churches
through secular channels. We may list, with Vatican I,
God's attributes: "omnipotent, eternal, immense, incompre-
hensible, infinite in understanding and will and every perfection . . . " and none can gainsay us. But such static descriptions make little impact on a world that is struggling
to survive. For many they may be true, but irrelevant.

This brings us back once more to the "death of God."
Secularization and dechristianization may seem to have made
God redundant; theologians of this school seem to have by-
passed the logical link between God and Christ in their
attempts to establish some form of Christian living on the
image of Christ for a world come of age. Still, they have
stated the modern dilemma in the starkest terms; they have
crystalized for us the process of purification of the sacred
by withdrawing unworthy notions of God; they have, as a
byproduct, led theologians to a renewed investigation of
God's action through his Spirit among secular realities. God
is wider than the Church and, as Teilhard de Chardin has
observed, "it is in no way metaphorical to say that man finds
himself capable of experiencing and discovering his God in
the whole length, breadth, and depth of the world in movement." Modern man may not use the word "God," but

"God" is only another name for the supreme Reality he is encountering.

Suggestions for further reading

Harvey Cox, *The Secular City* (New York: Macmillan, 1965); *The Secular City Debate*, ed. D. Callaghan (New York: Macmillan, 1966); Leslie Dewart, *The Future of Belief* (New York: Herder and Herder, 1966); T. W. Ogletree, *The Death of God Controversy* (Nashville: Abingdon Press, 1966); Sebastian Moore, *God Is a New Language* (London: Darton, Longman & Todd, 1967); Charles Davis, *God's Grace in History* (New York: Sheed & Ward, 1967).

5. Man in Nature and Grace

MAN'S EMERGENCE AND ORIGINAL SIN

"Leave me my ancestors in Paradise and I will allow you yours in the Zoological Gardens" — such an outraged reaction in the past century to Darwin's theory of evolution is unlikely to be widespread today. Despite Cardinal Manning's description of evolution as "a brutal philosophy — to wit, there is no God and the ape is our Adam," we have become accustomed to seeing the ape behind Adam, and the intricate calculation of the nineteenth century Cambridge scholar, John Lightfoot, that the actual creation of man took place on October 23, 4004 B.C. — at 9 a.m.! — appears as a laborious irrelevancy. Only a rugged fundamentalism would restrain our moderns from accepting the postulates of anthropology which sees man's origin as extending into a chiaroscuro of time when animal development and human origins seem to be inextricably confused.

The present general interest in the emergence of man — hominization — linked with the question of original sin (and, indeed, with sin in general) has arrived practically at the stage of after-dinner conversation and it may not be too much to hope to clarify here some notions on this topic. Further, our minds are becoming attuned to the realization that there is a universality of grace that is somehow tied up with man himself and not just a patent pending of the Church. Third, if grace is so linked to man in his own situation, how are we to view those earthly realities that go to make up so much of his existence in the light of his eternal destiny? Any "Christian Anthropology" that will form part of a future textbook of dogmatics must not ignore, then, these three basic considerations: (a) the process of hominization and the question of original sin; (b) the openness of man to grace; (c) the "theology of terrestrial realities."

Several works have been appearing in the past few years on the problem of man's origin and the complementary question of original sin. We have had the contributions of Dubarle and Schoonenberg and the major studies of Teilhard de Chardin and Karl Rahner. We may resume current thought on these investigations in six principal points: (1) God's plan comprised an evolution which stretched from early beginnings to be completed in a total human perfection. (2) The primordial created matter contained within itself an inbuilt impulse and orientation toward hominization, which would be arrived at after various stages — lasting milleniums — of the process of evolution. (3) When the actual process of hominization finally began, it did so in a gradual way, marked by an ebb and flow pattern: the first anthropoids would have been human rather in the sense that a child is human, yet without moral consciousness; a later group would have progressed to adulthood, with the capacity for personal decision and responsibility. (4) With the arrival of the first "adult," there was the demand, a challenge, to make a decision to follow conscience and accept God's love and rule — in other words, to make a supernatural "leap" from a purely natural existence. (5) This was refused and thus was impeded God's plan for man's evolution toward a total — and supernatural — perfection. Such a refusal from the emerging human race introduced sin into mankind. (6) This primeval, original sin established a state of "rebellion" which spread and deepened, each successive generation adding to it so that, finally, a complete environment of sin was experienced in the world. However, not to be balked by man's deviation, God renewed his plan for man's movement toward total perfection, to be achieved through union with him by means of Christ.

A number of queries must arise unbidden on the lips of many. Have we not here polygenism? Does this not deny the unity of the human race from Adam, and consequently the weakening (at least) of the doctrine of original sin, transmitted to all from one first parent? The hard core behind this objection is Romans 5:18–19: "Then as one man's trespass led to condemnation for all men, so one man's act of righteousness leads to acquittal and life for all men. For as by one man's disobedience many were made sinners, so by one man's obedience many will be made righteous." Paul's employment of the notion of "one man" (Adam) was taken from current thought pattern and was of use in so far as it served to contrast and so underline the all-embracing redemptive action of Christ for mankind, rather than as having an absolute value in itself. The unity of the human race — even if not wholly dependent on an "Adam" — is still maintained through God's placing of that impulse toward hominization in matter itself. The origin of our species still remains one. The account of "Adam" — Everyman — is the story of each man's response to God, and of the widening influence of the rejection of God's summons by sin.

Original sin would then be not only the early rejection of God's demand on man but the cumulative sin of the world into which all are born, by which all are influenced. Each man has deep down within him, prior to his personal acts and influencing them all, a reluctance to respond to God. The concept of the transmission of original sin through physical generation owes much to the feudal structure of privilege wherein privileges acquired by a father could be passed on to his heirs. If forfeited by the father, no entailment followed.

There may be one final query: what of the teaching on the immediate transfusion of a soul into the first man? Here, once more, we need not posit a miraculous intervention of God. Primordial matter, carrying within itself that impulse toward hominization when certain conditions were realized, would include such a natural "leap" within the very process of evolution. God's acts, to be effective, do not need to be immediate. His determination that hominization will be realized in one species at a given point and not in another is recognition enough that toward man he has exercised a particular intervention and effected an elevation of matter otherwise unattainable, as is evidenced in the brute creation with which we are surrounded.

NATURE AND GRACE

Now because of this early and all-embracing call of God to man to accept the overtures he was making to him in the depths of his conscience; because, too, of man's openness to that something beyond him, we are faced with newer insights into grace which have often received scant attention in our textbooks.

Man, precisely through this spiritual nature that is his, is — in sharp contrast to that brute creation which is confined to a limited sphere of action — open to the higher calling God has provided for him. His very nature is open to the supernatural, to grace. It has been the common assumption of our textbooks that grace is built on nature, very much as a superstructure, so that there is a clear distinction between "natural acts" and "supernatural acts." The consciousness of grace in everyday life, consequently, has been soft-pedaled if not completely overlooked. Yet grace permeates not only our essence but even our existence, the daily actions that make up our very lives. The New Testament speaks of the Spirit's action as "life," "anointing," "comfort," "light," as "groaning" — all far removed from a static, impersonal approach to man's experience of grace.

Human nature in the concrete is never "pure" nature, since nature is now subsumed into the supernatural order. As Karl Rahner has stated, "instead of placing the orders of redemption and creation alongside each other, we speak of the order of redemption *within* the order of creation" (*The Christian Commitment*, p. 60). Of course, this is not to say that the natural and the supernatural orders are one and the same thing, or that they are not distinct. But simply that the supernatural permeates all and creation finds its perfection and explanation in God's more embracing plan of man's elevation to the supernatural.

That is why there is such an intimate connection between the incarnation and the creation. The Word, coming into the world, makes the order of creation *his* order. The Thomist view that the incarnation took place to restore the balance upset by man's sin must give way before the Scotist view that God's love determined there would be an incarnation, and creation was to be the context in which this personal act of God's love would be shown. But it is of paramount importance to realize that the incarnation was not simply the Word taking flesh unto himself. God's plan for the incarnation included a previous stage wherein (principally in Israel) the realities of everyday life began to be assumed into a higher order of revelation — even elements from surrounding pagan religions could be taken over, once purified of their polytheism. With the incarnation itself it was not just that a human body became joined to a divine nature and a divine person; humanity itself received a definitive elevation with its earlier orientation toward God now firmly established. Further, all aspects of human existence were effectively placed within a supernatural context, the order of redemption. Man, since his appearance on this earth, has never been without the offer of grace: "All humanity receives that inward word of God calling men to a communion of grace with himself" (Schillebeeckx, *Christ the Sacrament*, p. 5).

Again, this is not to say that the natural and the supernatural order are one and the same thing, nor that the natural necessitated the supernatural. They remain distinct, but intimately linked, with the natural order directed to that fullness which is the union with God achieved in the supernatural. And what we dare not underestimate is that the actions which are part and parcel of what is often a domestic and humdrum existence are the very material for the supernatural sphere. The supernatural is not built upon the structure of our thought, words, and deeds; rather, it works precisely through them. We may even say that the supernatural is as wide (at least) as the natural order, with God's saving grace available to all men. God's meeting man, his self-gift to man, "uncreated grace" — which effects a change in man, "created grace" — is not confined to the visible Church, though this is the abiding sign of God's presence with man.

THEOLOGY OF EARTHLY REALITIES

This brings us to our third and final consideration of man in nature and grace: the "theology of terrestrial realities." In the 1930's a number of books dealing with Christian humanism began to appear (we may think of Christopher Dawson's *Progress and Religion*). Their theme was the relationship between nature and supernature, the continuing goodness of creation and created values despite sin, the natural link divinely contrived between creation and the life of grace. There was a preoccupation with "matter and spirit" which did not confine itself only to the literary, artistic, and philosophical values of human culture but took into account also questions of man in his work, his labors, his attempts to master his environment. This new approach to a Christian anthropology did not settle for a scholastic view of man as *animal rationale*, content to leave the matter there and move on to concentrate on his "spiritual life." Instead, man was considered in his entire temporal condition — the significance of his presence in the cosmos, his technical activity, his professional and civic relationships. At the side of some artificial writing on these topics, the studies of Jean Mouroux and Gustav Thils were erecting the first foundations for a theology of the body, of work, of progress, of social realities, etc. (An excellent though brief conspectus of these trends is to be found in the chapter on Roman Catholicism by the Louvain theologian, Roger Aubert, in *Twentieth Century Christianity*, edited by Bishop Stephen Neil.)

We are now aware how much such thought has played its part in Vatican II, as shown by the clear recognition in the document, *The Church in the Modern World*, of the positive values to be discerned in what may appear at first sight as merely secular trends among men of today. Teilhard de Chardin's view that, although man's final destiny belongs to a higher sphere, nevertheless his secular activities do contribute to the coming Kingdom of God is an appreciation of that incarnational theology which the Old and New Testaments exhibit. "Everything is grace," we have been told, and man, unless he clearly rejects God's overtures, can maintain that openness to the transcendent, to the supernatural, which God has instilled into him since his appearance in God's creation.

Suggestions for further reading

K. Rahner, Nature and Grace (New York: Sheed & Ward, 1963); P. Schoonenberg, God's World in the Making (Pittsburgh: Duquesne University Press, 1964); J. P. Mackey, Life and Grace (Dublin: Gill, 1966); Peter De Rosa, Christ and Original Sin (Milwaukee: Bruce, 1967); Rosemary Haughton, The Transformation of Man (London: G. Chapman, 1967).

6. Faith as Response to the Word of God

It may not be too much to suggest that for many of us
the treatise *De Fide* was one of the most arid and least
rewarding in the whole textbook course. We saw how the
Church decreed against Semi-Pelagianism that the first impulse to faith is a gift of God's grace; how faith, against
the Protestant notion of fiducial faith, is no mere confidence
but an assent to those things which God has both revealed
and promised; how, without the works of hope and love,
it is dead; how it is the start of salvation and the root of
all justification. Against nineteenth-century Rationalism we
read how the Church affirmed the supernatural and gratuitous
character of faith, as also its reasonableness.

We were introduced to the problems involved in the act
of faith. Were the preconditions of faith (*praeambula fidei*)
purely natural when the "beginning of faith" was itself an
interior grace of God? Was the act of faith fully and ade-
quately described as an act of the intellect, or should it not
more probably be described as engaging the whole human
person in its orientation toward God? We discussed, too,
what is believed (the material object of faith) and *why*
it is believed (the formal object). We learned, finally, how

faith is a theological virtue which enables man to accept the truth "connaturally," with a grasp of the detailed contents of faith based on a certain instinctive insight rather than on a process of logical analysis; this is equally true of the Church as a whole with its collective sense of the truth, the *sensus fidei*.

This was all very well as far as it went, but it did not go far enough. There was little appreciation of the unfolding notion of faith as a response to the word of God as found in the Scriptures, a complete misunderstanding of that *sola fides* slogan of the Reformers, and small attempt to show the total surrender involved in the person-to-person relationship established by faith. These three points may well call for comment.

FAITH AND THE WORD OF GOD

In chapter 11 of the Epistle to the Hebrews, the author sets out to show how the whole of Old Testament history is marked by faith. It is the very heart of religion, our link with God, that by which the unseen world (on which our own depends) becomes known to us. Because the writer is determined to find faith lived and preached throughout the whole of the Old Testament we may have expected to find "faith" written large on every one of its pages. What we do in fact find is that the Old Testament never mentions the noun "faith" at all. The nearest we seem to get is "faithfulness," "trustworthiness." St. Paul may quote Habakkuk 2:4: "The just man will live by faith" — but the Habakkuk text almost certainly means "a righteous man shall live by his fidelity," i.e. to God. As Weiser has shown in the *Theological Dictionary of the New Testament*, faith for the Old Testament meant faithfulness to the covenant concluded between God and his people. Under the influence of the prophetical movement (especially under the influence of Isaiah) and with personal experience and reflection, the depths of this relationship were sounded. Individual piety, mirrored in the

Psalms, was tutored by historical catastrophes and personal troubles. The significance of the Old Testament concept of faith lies in this that it is the expression of the particular form of existence, of day-to-day living, of the people of God who stood in an active relationship with God. Under threat to human existence, divine assurance releases fresh sources of faith and life. Hence faith can assume the meaning also of obedience to the will of God as revealed in the Law and of confession of the true God in confrontation with surrounding idolatry. The basis of Israel's confident steadfastness was the mighty deeds God had done for her.

When we come to the New Testament, we cannot fail to see that faith has a place which it never had before. If we want to know what fresh ideas and new convictions the Gospel introduced we cannot do better than study carefully the new words which the first Christians were obliged to coin. Among such words there appears the word "faith" (*pistis*). Donald Baillie, a noted Scottish theologian, described the early Christians of all schools as being "conscious of this great new thing which had come into their lives and spoke of it at every turn" (*Faith in God*, new edition, London, 1964, p. 36). In the Acts of the Apostles we find Christianity repeatedly designated simply as "the faith," with "believers" as a common name for those who, accepting the preaching of the apostles, joined the Christian community.

It is true that, if we turn to the Synoptic Gospels to look for the teaching of Christ on this subject, we shall be disappointed. There is no discussion of faith as an abstract term. The word occurs rather as a rule in very practical connections — healing, casting out devils, the resurrection of the dead, Christ's preaching. The one religious disposition which Christ did emphasize was faith, the believing disposition. When people stood helpless before the difficulties of everyday life it was because they were lacking in faith.

St. John and St. Paul develop a very extensive theology of faith — Paul in the light of the Jewish notion of the Law as means of salvation, John from the point of view of Christ present in the sacramental life of the Church. A glance at Paul's letters will show how he could hardly write a page on any subject without using the word faith: the noun occurs over one hundred times in his letters — in Galatians and Romans over sixty times, and even the small note to Philemon mentions faith twice. Paul's principal concern is to show how faith is the root of justification and not those works prescribed by the Law. Since Christ came, it is faith in him, acceptance of him, and surrender to him that justifies man and calls forth the process of repentance and salvation. The Johannine literature presents a curious mixture of evidence: so strange that the Fourth Gospel, which takes so much delight in abstract terms like "truth," "light," "life," etc., should have made no use of the word "faith." In fact, the Fourth Gospel and 2 and 3 John are the only books of the New Testament where the word does not occur. In 1 John we do read "this is the victory that overcomes the world, our faith." And, in the Gospel the verb "to believe" is given a very prominent place to express one of the main ideas of the book: the means of sharing in the life offered by the Father and Christ. Faith in the Son brings life; he who does not believe is already condemned. Faith establishes our relationship with Father, Son, and Holy Spirit. And in both John and Paul faith is linked to baptism and repentance.

The famous text of Hebrews 11:1: "Now faith is the assurance of things hoped for, the conviction of things not seen," describes faith in a more intellectualistic way than that found in the rest of the New Testament and it has proved a boon to speculative theologians who have treated faith as just an act of the intellect. However, it should not be separated from the more personal aspect exhibited in the rest of the New Testament: the intellect may be involved in the adhesion of faith, but the whole person, too. And, according to Hebrews, the Christian, with the host of witnesses from the Old Testament, should fix his eyes on Jesus who initiates faith and brings it to completion: "the pioneer and perfector of our faith" (12:2).

The remaining New Testament writings also have their treatment of faith, but of peculiar interest is the discussion in James 2:14–20 of faith and works. We may take it that James thought Paul's views on freedom from the law needed further explanation among Jewish Christians. Some people may have thought that freedom from the law meant freedom from all obligations. James insists that faith without works is dead, and he goes on to list practical considerations which must involve any Christian. We have been so preoccupied with reconciling James and Paul that we have often failed to notice that Paul did neglect to place "good works" in relationship to faith, so concerned was he to establish the justifying role of faith.

In the New Testament, then, faith becomes the be-all and end-all. Christianity is faith: in God, in Jesus, in the apostolic proclamation. It is faith in a person rather than in a creed — this latter only follows from acceptance of a person. It is opposed to the Law, to works, as the one means of justification. It lives through works but it is above them. It is a total surrender in response to the God who made himself known in Jesus Christ.

JUSTIFICATION BY FAITH

Mention of faith and justification must naturally evoke the figure of Luther with his cry of *sola fides* as the one means of achieving righteousness in the sight of God. We must not underestimate the very real contribution made by the Reformers in insisting on the pivotal role of faith in man's salvation. Counter-Reform polemics have led to mis-understanding, with almost perverse hardening of views on both sides. Hans Küng, in his *Justification* (pp. 237–253), has dealt at some length with this whole question. He shows how the controversy began in 1521 when Luther translated Romans 3:28 as, "That a man be justified . . . by faith alone." The formula *sola fides*, even before the Reformation, could be found in Catholic translations (one German and three

Italian), in eight Fathers, in St. Thomas (commenting on 1 Tim 1:8). But what of its meaning? Louis Bouyer (*Protestantism*, pp. 12–13) explains:

> That faith *alone* saves us means, if it means anything, that we on our part must add nothing to it, nothing outside it or independent of it. Any such addition would necessarily result in a negation of the essential, for if, though believing in principle in the saving action of God, we felt constrained to add anything at all in which we would rely on our own initiative, what would be the result? We would fall back at once into the impossible situation from which grace had rescued us; we would have to accomplish one part of our salvation, trusting to God to do the rest. But our actual state of wretchedness comes from our incapacity for any effective initiative, even incomplete, in regard to salvation; in short, we have not only to be assisted in order to save ourselves, but in order to be saved. . . . Now precisely that insight of Luther which is preserved in the type of Protestantism most faithful to its origins and most truly Christian, is that *all* is grace, and that, consequently, *all* in our salvation comes to us by faith.

That is why Paul always links justification with faith, and not with love. No kind of work, not even a work of love, justifies man, but faith alone. This is no mere confidence (*fiducia*), nor a simple intellectual adhesion to abstract truths. Rather, it is the affirmation of a person, Christ, to whom one is now fully dedicated. Consequently, there is a living community of will between the believer and Christ: it is a living faith, not a faith which stands over against, and opposed to, works. And this faith which is the beginning of salvation can never be abandoned during this lifetime. It is also (as Moehler, the past-century theologian, remarked) "the continuing foundation on which the whole structure of salvation is being erected."

The Protestant charge against us of "moralism versus justification" has some truth in it. In our anxiety to emphasize the necessity of works, our view of the all-embracing action of God — even when we do perform good works — has not always been as total as might have been expected. We have considered ourselves partial causes with God of our own merit, forgetting that our efforts have really been embedded in his. It would be easy, too (if space permitted), to trace the consequences of this blurring of vision in those individualistic forms of devotion which focus on the prayer of the dévot to the detriment of the central liturgy with its emphasis on the saving action of Christ.

FAITH AS PERSONAL SURRENDER

We may now turn to the implications involved in the person-to-person surrender of faith. The biblical data shows that the object of faith is not a series of truths but a person, Christ himself. It is true that in the Synoptic Gospels an object of faith is not generally stated. Faith alone, as a religious attitude, is demanded. We are being asked to commit ourselves to something not closely defined; there is something absolute about the demand, a demand for surrender without anything being withheld. We are being asked to submit fully to this new era that is polarized around the central character: to the kingdom of God here and now manifested in this person who proclaims the rule of God anew and who is in fact the autobasileia, the kingdom itself. There is to be an as yet unexplored surrender (is there not something of this in ordination to the priesthood and religious profession?). Consequent on this surrender demanded by faith are a number of sequelae. Faith introduces and establishes, we have noted, a personal relationship with Christ. He is redeemed man incorporate and our redemption depends on the degree of union we achieve with him. We cease to exist as a detached unit of humanity. When man falls he falls alone, but his salvation is arrived at within the community of the redeemed. The Acts of the Apostles show how closely this community of believers is identified with the exalted Lord who now lives and works through his Spirit. If besides Jesus the object of faith is the proclamation of the Gospel, yet this very proclamation renders the Lord

Jesus present to the believing community. In the proclamation of the Word he is present.

Within this community of faith are received the sacraments which have a unique place because they are wholly, and in a fashion nothing else is, the essence of salvation and signs of faith. "They not only presuppose faith, but by words and objects they also nourish, strengthen and express it; that is why they are called 'sacraments of faith'" (*Constitution on the Liturgy*, art. 59). Through faith and the sacraments of faith we enter into a dialogue with the Word in the assembled community.

Yet faith in its action is not confined to a properly Christian environment; it throws new light on life. "The People of God believes that it is led by the Spirit of the Lord, who fills the earth. Motivated by this faith it labors to decipher authentic signs of God's presence and purpose in the happiness, needs, and desires in which this people has a part along with other men of our age. For faith throws a new light on everything, manifests God's designs for man's total vocation, and thus directs the mind to solutions which are fully human" (*Church in the Modern World*, art. 11). Faith will show its fruitfulness in the believer by penetrating his whole life, including its worldly dimensions. To the believer who has encountered Christ there is an increasing knowledge of self that is far more than a psychological by-product. More meaning is given to life, insecurity replaced by security, and there is a growth in strength and power. Only in that final and uninterrupted union with Christ will faith come to its full perfection. It will not pass away (St. Paul has been misread at 1 Cor 13:13) but will become a response of the whole person to the Word of God.

Suggestions for further reading

K. H. Schelkle, *The Epistle to the Romans* (New York: Herder and Herder, 1964); J. L. McKenzie, *The Power and the Wisdom* (Milwaukee: Bruce, 1965), particularly ch. 8; P. Babin, *Crisis of Faith* (Dublin: Gill, 1965); C. Cirne-Lima, *Personal Faith* (New York: Herder and Herder, 1965).

7. The Church in Her Mystery

It has become current in the past few decades to speak of a renewal in the study of the Church, ecclesiology, among both Catholics and those of the Lutheran and Reform traditions (the late Lutheran Bishop, Dibelius, has called our century "the century of the Church"). Since the Counter-Reform, a bureaucratic ecclesiology had developed among us, interfering with New Testament and patristic notions of the Church which were more profound and more realistic. The reaction a hundred years ago from the Tübingen theologian, John Adam Moehler (to whom Newman acknowledged his debt), and from another scholar of the same school more known to English readers, Karl Adam writing in the 1920's, was little felt in the Anglo-Saxon world. With *Mystici Corporis*, a more theological and less juridical approach to the nature of the Church made an *official* entrance into ecclesiology through a development of the idea of the Church as being the Body of Christ. (It is astounding, when we come to think of it, how — as Leo Trese remarks in his *Vessels of Clay* — earlier textbooks of this century serving the older priests of our time told their readers nothing of the Church as the Mystical Body of Christ.)

Biblical and liturgical studies carried forward the teaching

47

of Pius XII, and Vatican II has given us further valuable material for investigation. Whereas previously there had been a rather one-sided emphasis on the hierarchical structure of the Church, now there is also a greater realization of the complex depth, fullness, and richness of the Church — her "mystery" (a word covering more than intellectual ignorance before a truth of our faith).

The recent Constitution on the Church has an important opening chapter on the "Mystery of the Church," but for a fuller appreciation of all this two other chapters on the "People of God" (ch. 2) and the "Pilgrim Church" (ch. 7) must be considered. From these chapters we may attempt an examination of certain notions which are fruitful for understanding the divine-human reality, the saving event that is the Church. It has to be admitted that in reading these three chapters one finds an overlapping and repetition of ideas. The present pages can only offer to underline two principal suggestions on the Church in her mystery. (For further study of the actual Constitution there are available a number of commentaries, perhaps those of Gregory Baum and Austin Flannery being the most accessible to English-speaking readers.) The two ideas that are so novel in the Constitution are the Church in her mystery as being a "sign" and a "pilgrim people." Other aspects treated of the Church, such as the Body of Christ, the fourfold imagery of the flock of Christ (pastoral), the vineyard of God (agri-cultural), the temple of the Spirit (building), and the spouse of the immaculate Lamb (bridal), are to be seen in relation to the basic New Testament notion of the Church as the People of God. They shall be referred to here insofar as they serve to underline or contrast treatment of the Church as the People of God.

SIGN OF GOD'S PRESENCE IN THE WORLD

The Church is called "a kind of sacrament or sign of intimate union with God, and of the unity of all mankind" (art. 1). One of the most thought-provoking reflections on this first article has been given by Karl Rahner in *The Christian of the Future*, a paper read to the Catholic Students Association of Freiburg University (Germany) during the Church Unity Octave of 1965. He sees this text as one that demands inclusion in any future Denziger, and comments:

> For Christendom in earlier times, the Church was the one plank of salvation in the shipwreck of the world, the small barque on which alone men are saved, the small band of those who are saved by the miracle of grace from the *massa damnata*, and the *extra ecclesiam nulla salus* was understood in a very exclusive and pessimistic way.
>
> But in this conciliar text the Church is not the society of those who alone are saved, but the sign of the salvation of those who, as far as its historical and social structure is concerned, do not belong to it. By their profession of faith, their worship and their life, the human beings in the Church form as it were the one expression in which the hidden grace promised and offered to the whole world emerges from the abysses of the human soul into the domain of history and society.

Despite the diaspora being created by growing secularization and diminishing Christianity, the Church, even if she lose her discernible external features to the world, still remains the primal sign of God's saving grace, real and effective, among men. She must ever be "the dynamic representative minority that is spiritually responsible for the final destiny of all" (Yves Congar, *The Wide World, My Parish*, p. 12). On account of this sign of God's hidden presence in the world, men as yet unacquainted with Christian revelation, and even those who have not yet arrived at an explicit belief in God himself, may, by the grace of Christ, reach salvation if they accept the impulses of grace God is granting to them. They too are called to form part of his people. Because of this, there is much truth in the suggestion that one of the most important lines of thought to be followed in a treatise *De Ecclesia* is anthropological: man in grace

and nature — a theme which is taken up enthusiastically by
the *Church in the Modern World.*

Thus a wider foundation is laid for the notion of the
Church as the people of God than to confine it simply to
a select and separate Old or New Testament élite. Vocation
and grace were extended beyond the boundaries of such a
nucleus: this dynamic minority is representative of God's
action in the world and man's response to it. All humanity
is destined to become attached to that creative center which
is the people of God.

A PEOPLE

Begun by the Father in the Old Testament, founded by
the Son in the New, vitalized and renewed by the Spirit
of Pentecost, this people of God shines forth as "a people
made one with the unity of the Father, the Son, and the
Holy Spirit" (art. 4): its origin lies linked with the Trinity
itself. Various pointers from the Old and New Testaments
help us to define the characteristics of this people. There
is the notion of solidarity — one nation, an overall tradition
which allows for a plurality of local practices, one head. And
(more than in the image of the Church as the Body of
Christ) there is contained the idea of each individual pre-
serving intact his personality, receiving in full liberty the
grace of God to grow into full maturity in Christ. On the
social plane, the notion of a people admits of the inclusion
of good and bad in the Church as in Israel. The teeming
impoverished millions who are also called to be part of
that people warn us that a characteristic of that same people
must be poverty. Then, the image of the people of God
bears on the relationship of baptized Christians to the
Catholic Church. This requires some comment.

Pius XII, in *Mystici Corporis,* had described Catholics
as being "really" (*reapse*) members of the Body of Christ.
The background of this thought was the Church as a social
body. The present Constitution, considering the Body of

Christ rather as a communion of life with Christ in a fellowship enlivened by the gifts of the Spirit, sees Catholics as "fully" incorporated into this union with Christ. This implies that the Body of Christ is wider than the Catholic Church in which it "subsists" (art. 8). There is clear recognition that "elements of sanctification and of truth can be found outside of her visible structure. These elements, however, as gifts properly belonging to the Church of Christ, possess an inner dynamism toward Catholic unity" (art. 8). The Constitution goes on to look at some of these (as also does the Decree on Ecumenism, art. 3). Non-Catholic Christians thus belong in some way to the Body of Christ, but, as Avery Dulles has remarked in the *Documents of Vatican II*, edited by Walter Abbott, p. 33: "By treating the relationship of the other Christians to the Catholic Church under the heading of the 'people of God' rather than that of the 'Mystical Body,' the Constitution is able to avoid various subtle and controversial questions concerning 'degrees of membership' which have been much discussed since the time of *Mystici Corporis*." Hence such Christians do form part of the Body of Christ, do belong to the people of God, are members of the Church of Christ, yet without that fullness that the Catholic Church possesses.

PROPHETICAL, PRIESTLY, ROYAL

To return to the image of the people of God: here, prior to any distinction between "clergy and laity," is the sharing through baptism, which effects incorporation into Christ's Body, of Christ's triple office of priest, prophet, and king. The common or universal priesthood of the faithful permits Christians to share effectively in Christ's ministry through the liturgy and sacraments. These are not to be considered simply as acts of individuals but as ecclesial events, articulating and making actual the self-realization of the Church: they help the Church become what she is in herself. In public, communal worship the life of the entire Church is being built up, and her grace-giving function from Christ's own priesthood is made realizable before the world.

To the role of Christ as prophet corresponds the office of witness in the Church. This role of bearing witness is exercised in the liturgy and in the various manifestations of the Church's teaching. It is also exercised in a particular way through the *sensus fidelium* by which the whole Church, laity as well as hierarchy, live, meditate on, and render explicit the life of truth in the Church — a continual bearing witness to the Gospel by all. (In the last century Newman's article in *The Rambler* of 1859, "On consulting the laity in matters of doctrine," made this point — and caused a completely unjustified scandal!) The charismatic influence of the Spirit is to be found in all, even if it is not made explicit through those spectacular phenomena recorded in the period of the apostolic Church.

Mirroring the universal Lordship of Christ the King, the Church exhibits a common fellowship within her commonwealth and is committed to bringing all men into this communion under Christ. In so doing she respects the thought forms, culture, and everyday life of all nations, demanding no rigid uniformity to one pattern.

We may present this relationship between Christ and the people of God thus:

Christ:	priest	prophet	king
Hierarchy:	sanctifying	teaching	governing
Faithful:	ministry	witness	fellowship
The New Testament's:	*diakonia*	*marturion*	*koinonia*

PILGRIMS AND SINNERS

Now because this people of God, "like a pilgrim in a foreign land, presses forward amid the persecutions of the world and the consolations of God" (the words are St. Augustine's), found "in poverty and under oppression" (art. 8), there is a human situation within the Church which includes the presence of sin: the Church in her concrete historical existence here below, made up of defectible human beings, is ever in need of purification and renewal, *ecclesia semper reformanda.* The Church should show forth the holiness of her Founder, but if she does not do so "she should reform herself, correct herself, make herself recover that conformity with her divine model which is her fundamental duty" (Pope Paul, in his *Allocutio* to the Second Session, September 29, 1963). The same Holy Father referred to the "Church of Penitence."

Time was when such admission would seem (at least to textbook theology) almost heretical. Was not the Church all holy, the work of the Holy Spirit? Other Christian bodies saw personal penitence and ecclesial penitence as basically one penitence since for them the institutional forms of the Church, being works of faith under God's grace, would still be human and thus defectible, the Church not yet having arrived at that stage of fulfillment designed by God. At the Council, Cardinal Bea criticized an earlier draft of the document on the Church for not distinguishing the eschatological or final Church — which is utterly holy — from the pilgrim Church which works for the sanctity of its members while embracing sinners. If the Church had been holy without qualification in the sixteenth century, there would have been no Reformation.

But the pilgrim Church is one with Christ in his carnal state in which something of sin, though not sin itself, was associated with his mortality. "This association with sin touches not only Christ's mortal condition but also the personal commitment of his human existence as his acceptance of the baptism of John and his reference to the Passion as a baptism can be interpreted" (John Thornhill, "The Pilgrim Church and Penitence for Christian Disunity," an excellent article in the *Clergy Review* of January, 1965). Evidently there is (unlike for Christ) more than mere association with sin in the Church, despite that essential holiness of hers. This holiness does not prevent, here and now, the presence of sin in the Church through her members, and thus, here and now, a marring of the Church by sin. Fr. Cornelius Ernst has remarked (in reference to the Herbert McCabe affair): "In these texts from Vatican II we may notice that although the Church itself is never called sinful, it is the Church itself which is said to be in constant need of purification and renewal. The Church has always been accused of the sins of her members; she is not without spot or wrinkle, since in the interpretation of Ephesians 5:27 adopted in the last of the conciliar texts quoted above [he is referring to the Decree on Ecumenism, art. 4] it is only in her final glory that she will be entirely purified . . . and also the historical pilgrim Church of the faithful People of God striving to overcome sin" (*The Purification of the Church*, p. 25). The same writer remarks how the problem of sin in the Church is real and serious, and not to be evaded simply because it is theologically difficult or because it requires us to face uncomfortable facts. Thus chapter seven of the Constitution can deal specifically with this tension existing between the present pilgrim Church and her final realization. (This chapter was included at the insistence of Pope John.) The New Testament writings themselves show a tension between an already achieved salvation and the perfect fulfillment that is still to come, and it is not always easy to reconcile such texts unless we recognize how salvation, though won by Christ, has still to be realized in each person. The Christians addressed in 2 Peter 3:12 are, by their good lives, "waiting for and hastening the coming of the day of the Lord."

That is why finally we still await the complete establishment of God's Kingdom, his saving rule. The rule of God has not yet full sway among us and so the Church and the Kingdom of God do not yet coincide: the Church is the Kingdom of God in the state of becoming. During his earthly life, Jesus grouped together and educated disciples to whom he revealed the mysteries of the Kingdom; they were to form the beginning of a new people who would be the domain in which God's royal rule would be exercised. In Christ himself the dominion of God found an obedient man and so God's Kingdom was fully manifested. Christ indeed was the Kingdom of God made visible. But, just as in Israel, men are not prepared to submit fully to the demands God is making, even within the Church. Thus, although God's Kingdom was established in Christ, only at the end of time will it be perfectly realized among men when all things are restored in Christ. The quest of God to bring man once more under his saving and sanctifying rule will then be achieved. The people of God, the Church, the Kingdom — call it what we will — shall have at last realized the universal salvific will of God to bring all men into enduring union with him.

Suggestions for further reading

Yves Congar, *The Mystery of the Temple* (Westminster, Md.: Newman, 1962); ———— *The Mystery of the Church* (London: G. Chapman, 1965); J. Guitton, *The Church and the Laity: from Newman to Vatican II* (Staten Island: Alba House, 1965); *The Purification of the Church*, ed. Ian Hislop (London: SCM Press, 1967); K. Rahner, *The Christian of the Future* (New York: Herder and Herder, 1967); *The Evolving Church*, ed. D. Flanagan (Staten Island: Alba House, 1967).

8. The Church in Her Structure

In the last century W. G. Ward said he would like to have a papal bull every day with his *Times* at breakfast; the pope was spoken of as the "vice-God of humanity"; breviary hymns addressed to God were redirected to Pio Nono; a Jesuit review (to which Pius IX subscribed) stated that when the pope meditated, God was thinking in him; a leading French bishop spoke of the pope as the continuation of the Incarnate Word; the Archbishop of Reims could protest against "an idolatry of the papacy." These examples (quoted by Alec Vidler in *The Church in an Age of Revolution*, pp. 153–154) of the spirit of the times surrounding Vatican I with its definition of papal primacy and infallibility give weight to the charge of Roman Catholic papalism: the pope, and the pope alone, mattered. But the *Schemata* prepared for Vatican I included texts on the nature of the episcopal office, a counterbalance to its teaching on the papal office. The day after 533 bishops had cast their votes in favor of that teaching on the papacy the Franco-Prussian war broke out. Italian armies invaded the Papal States, Rome capitulated, and the temporal power of the papacy was brought to an end. Such an accident of history was responsible for leaving the doctrine on the structure of the Church suspended in midair. The political upheaval forced a postponement of the Council *sine die*, and we have had to wait a century to gain an overall view of that structure.

Vatican II was not content merely to examine the episcopal office. It took up also questions on the function of the priesthood, the diaconate, and the laity in the Church, thus giving us important doctrinal affirmations for renewed theological investigations. It would not be sufficient, if one would know the Council's teaching on bishops, priests, deacons, and laity, to consult chapter three — pivotal though it may be — of the Constitution on the Church. There are also the decrees on the Bishops' Pastoral Office, on the Ministry and Life of Priests, on Priestly Formation; and, besides the Constitution's chapter four on the laity, there is the Decree on the Apostolate of the Laity. Other documents also touch upon these questions in practical matters (e.g., the Constitution on the Liturgy). In the following pages an attempt will be made to summarize the new perspectives recognized by Vatican II on the structure of the Church and then to indicate the problems in theology which surround the Council's statements.

BISHOPS

First of all, as to the bishops. Two principal doctrines are affirmed: the sacramentality of episcopal consecration and the collegiality of the bishops. Within the background of the notion of the people of God, the Constitution explains hierarchical authority in the Church as a service for — not as dominion over — the people of God: "these ministers who are endowed with sacred power are servants of their brethren" (art. 18). The office of bishop started with Christ forming the apostles into "a college or a fixed group" (art. 19), giving them collective powers and functions for the proclamation of the Gospel and for the ordering of the primitive Church. The doctrine of Vatican I is reaffirmed on the primacy of Peter among the apostles, now extended to the primacy and infallibility of the pope as Peter's successor. The bishops are seen as the successors of the apostles, with that supreme authority in the Church which the apostles possessed. The link between the apostles and the bishops having been made, the Constitution takes up the question of the sacramentality of the episcopal office: "This sacred Synod teaches that by episcopal consecration is conferred the fullness of the sacrament of orders" (art. 21). By his consecration the bishop receives the fullness of the powers of orders. He is not just a priest with extended powers of jurisdiction but he now receives permanent and inalienable powers to sanctify, teach, and govern the Church, these powers to be exercised in "hierarchical communion" with the pope and the bishops in union with him.

Mention of "hierarchical communion" introduces the second and most important doctrinal affirmation of chapter three of the Constitution: the "collegiality" of the bishops. (We have seen this at work in the Council, and the Synod of Bishops, promised by Paul VI in his motu proprio of September 15, 1965, and held in October, 1967, was one of the forms of appropriate "collegiate action" referred to in art. 22.)

The Constitution is careful to explain, both in the text itself and in notes appended to the document that necessarily and always the college of bishops includes the idea of a head who preserves intact in the college his role of Vicar of Christ and shepherd of the universal Church. We are not to consider the duality pope-bishops, but rather pope-pope and bishops: the pope by himself and the pope together with the bishops collectively. He alone as head of the college can perform certain acts which in no way are under the competence of the bishops, e.g., convoking and directing the college, approving norms of action, etc. In every instance of collegial action it is clear that the union of the bishops with the pope is demanded. Obviously, while the college of bishops is a permanent institution, still, as tradition shows, it does not always operate through strictly collegial action. This will be found only at intervals, such as during the Council itself. The college is the subject of supreme and full power over the whole Church. But residential bishops (other than the pope) exercise actual government only over their particular church. Nevertheless their pastoral solicitude, as members of the episcopal college, extends to the whole Church. Practical consequences of this touch the missions, needy dioceses, territorial episcopal conferences — points developed at some length in the Decree on the Bishops' Pastoral Office.

To complete its treatment of the role of bishops, the Constitution examines in their regard the prophetic, priestly, and kingly functions of Christ. Answering to the prophetic or teaching office of the individual bishop for his own church, a "religious assent" is demanded from his flock which is to be seen within the framework of that total submission due to the infallible teaching of the whole college of bishops or to papal *ex cathedra* statements. Such religious assent may be to noninfallible teaching. In his priestly function, because the mystery of the whole Church is made present and actualized in the celebration and regulation of the eucharist in the local church, the bishop maintains the unity of the Church. The eucharist, more than any other sacrament, signifies and effects that unity. Lastly, in his government of his diocese — a sharing in Christ's kingly office — the bishop acts by his own authority and not merely as a delegate of the pope.

PRIEST AND DEACONS

To understand something of what the Council has to say about priests, one has to turn to the Decree on the Ministry and Life of Priests. This document had a checkered history, the earlier proposals of 1963 and 1964 being returned as too meager and inadequate, a bare list of propositions. The present document takes as its principle that the priest is a man chosen from among the people of God to be sealed in the very depths of his being by a consecration of the Holy Spirit which makes him like to Christ and deputes him to serve the people of God. There is one eternal priesthood, one mission, which Christ received from the Father. This was communicated in a special way to the apostles and to their successors, the bishops. Through these latter the priest derives in a dependent fashion his participation in the priesthood of Christ. No mere "cult man" standing apart from the community at the altar, the priest shares in Christ's triple function: prophetic, by his ministry of the Word; priestly, by his ministry of the sacraments, particularly the eucharist; kingly, by his ministry of ruling the people of God, a sign of the bishop to whom this task is communicated in an eminent way.

Chapter two of the document deals with this question of the ministry of the priest in some detail, emphasizing his role of service for the people of God. The "root and hinge" of the Christian community is the celebration of the eucharist, yet it is the ministry of the Word that demands the priest's first attention: in proclaiming that Word, in instruction that makes it relevant to our time, in his living of it, the priest, through the Word, gathers together God's people who are then nourished in the Liturgy. His priesthood is primarily ministerial through Word and Sacrament, and within this role the cultic aspect of sacrifice is to be placed. Because of this all-embracing ministry (chapter 3), Christ lives and acts in the priest; it is his first and irreducible road to sanctity. External ministry and interior spirituality are fused into one "pastoral charity" through the Eucharistic Sacrifice, the focus of a total ministry which includes the priest's own sanctification.

Article 29 of the Constitution on the Church, which provided for the restoration of the diaconate as a grade of orders in its own right (and not merely as a step to the priesthood), has been implemented by *Sacrum Diaconatus Ordinem* of June 27, 1967. According to this *motu proprio*, the permanent diaconate is to be established on a local basis, depending on the episcopal conferences and subject to the approval of Rome. It may be conferred on men who undertake to remain unmarried and are over the age of 25. A married man who is over 35 may be ordained. There is to be a three-year trial period before ordination.

THE LAITY

Finally, the laity. The usual distinction between "clergy and laity" is a secondary one, one which must give precedence to the basic fact, established by baptism, that *all* the members of the Church enjoy a universal priesthood and have an active role to play in the people of God. For the laity this active role has the form of a mission to the secular world: "A secular quality is proper and special to laymen" (art. 31) — a point developed in the decree on the Church in the Modern World. An earlier view of the lay apostolate had reduced it to the status of errand-boy service for the clergy in their apostolic tasks. Chapter four of the Constitution on the Church (as well as the decree on the Apostolate of the Laity) insists on the laity possessing their own proper and peculiar role in the Church in a mutual relationship of support and dependence with the clergy. "Familiar dialogue" (art. 37) should imply the presence of the laity in discussions at parochial, diocesan, and even Council level.

Like bishops and priests, the laity share in the triple role of Christ: priestly, by their efforts to consecrate the secular world to God its creator; prophetic, by their role of witnesses stemming from baptism and confirmation, enlivened by the charisms bestowed on them by the Spirit for the promotion of Christian truth and life both inside and outside the Church; kingly, by contributing to the rule of God in everyday life, not only in the field of faith and morals but even in the progress of civilization and culture.

THEOLOGICAL PROBLEMS

Such, in simple outline, is the doctrine proposed by the Council on the Church in her structure. However, there is a mass of theological problems underlying this matter — questions on an "institutionalized Church"; on authority and freedom; on the relationship of the Petrine office and the papal office; on the tension between monarchical-papal and hierarchical-episcopal structure; on the continuity between the apostolic and the ecclesiastical offices; on the fluidity in the New Testament writings between *episcopos* and *presbyteros*, between presbyter and layman, and as to whether the primitive community was ruled by monarchical bishops or by a college of presbyters; on the actual conferring of office; on the differentiating of grades within one sacrament and their specific institution by Christ; on the "representative" function of the minister; on cultic versus ministerial priesthood; on "women priests."

We may approach such a snarl of problems in the following fashion. There is in the Church a sacrament of leadership with a rite conferring office and its corresponding grace. There are also in the Church free charisms which are not interchangeable with office. Christ has conferred office on the Church *en bloc*, as it were, but it is left to the Church to exercise transmission of office even to the extent of conferring only certain powers at any one time. This "partial" transmission of office still remains a sacrament. It is difficult to show that a distinction between the episcopal and the priestly office was made by Christ: it comes rather from the Church (Trent defined that the hierarchy as a whole, however, exists *ordinatione divina*). The disputed question as to whether a priest receives in its entirety the power of orders (we can think of parish priests confirming, of the likelihood of power to ordain being given here and there in the Middle Ages to simple priests), so that the rite of episcopal consecration would be a sacramental, seems to have been definitively solved by

Vatican II with its teaching on the episcopal office. As to deacons, these too (as we have noted earlier) would be a grade of the same sacrament of orders, established in its own right with its own particular grace of state.

If we trace our steps back to the New Testament to discover the precise relationship between the various grades of orders we shall be disappointed. We do find a special function conferred on Peter and the beginnings of the apostolic college. This apostolic office, foundational as it is and essential to the transmission of revelation itself, is unique. It is true that the functions of *episcopos* and *presbyteros* seem often to be interchangeable, but this does not detract from the central issue that a leadership under apostolic guidance stands out. The close of the apostolic era did not dispense with the Petrine and apostolic tasks: preaching, the sacraments, government still had to go on: there had to be continuity between the apostolic and the ecclesiastical office.

We are getting "apostolic succession." Yet this succession is to be understood in the sense of a pope succeeding to the Petrine office and bishops to the apostolic college qua college (not as successors to individual apostles). This notion of apostolic succession is nothing new to Anglicanism, but Küng has examined how "in the past few years many Protestant theologians have voiced a positive and constructive opinion about the question of apostolic succession" (*Structures of the Church*, p. 152; cf. his comments on the 1957 Report of the German Lutheran Church in *A Declaration concerning the Apostolic Succession, ibid.*, pp. 154–156).

As to the problem involving the tension between the monarchical-papal and the hierarchical-episcopal structure in the Church, Rahner (*Theology for Renewal*, pp. 12–26) believes that it should be approached from the angle of the Church as "universal" and yet "local." The Church, that is, the whole Church, becomes fully tangible in *this* local Church, principally through the celebration of the eucharist. The local Church is not simply an agency of the universal

Church but here and now makes present that universal Church. Over such local Churches preside the individual bishops. But to preserve universal unity and maintain the totality of the local Churches, one center of unity is essential: the pope. Last year we heard San Francisco's Episcopalian Bishop Myers appealing that "we need the Pope, because in this perilous age we need one symbolically potent bishop to give expression to the word of the Lord for our day." Thus while the bishop governs his own Church with his own autonomy, while the college of bishops governs the universal Church with the Pope, the Petrine primacy ensures an overall leadership that links together organically — not merely juridically — the totality of the local Churches.

In the election of such local heads of Churches we are becoming increasingly aware of a demand for a certain "democratization": the procedure of choosing a *trina* should give way to a consultation of clergy and laity. Whatever may be valid in this demand should not obscure the fact that the conferring of office comes from Christ, not from the "people" — even the people of God. Democratization of spiritual office under the older Luther led quickly to its devaluation and a one-sided emphasis on the "representative" role of the ministry ignored the interior consecration effected by the Spirit on the ordained subject. It was inevitable that Luther should write his tract against the "invented *characteres indelibiles.*"

Mention of "ministry" evokes the further question of the relation of cultic and ministerial priesthood. The main emphasis in Catholic theology (at least since the Reformation, which whittled down and finally dispensed with the sacrificial aspect of the Mass) has been on the cultic function of the priesthood: a priest was a man ordained to sacrifice. But, as we have already noted, the role of the priest is primarily ministerial — the ministry of Word and Sacrament. In this ministry a peak is reached in the eucharistic celebration, the apogee of Word and Sacrament.

Women priests, finally. If we can put aside our prejudices,

theoretical and practical, we may one day decide that there are no scriptural or theological reasons why women should not be ordained, although tradition, as manifested in the practice of the Church, is not encouraging.

While we await the putting into effect of *Sacram Diaconatus Ordinem*, aware of the apostolic endeavors of laymen, we may well meditate on these words of Karl Rahner (*Theology for Renewal*, p. 66):

> Those who share in this way in the Church's hierarchical apostolate, exercising part of the function of the hierarchy's mission, given that they do so on a permanent, full-time basis, are not, to be theologically precise, really laymen, even if they have received no "ordination" in the usual sense. They belong to the clergy. The real significance of their vocation and commissioning for their office (extra-canonical and extra-liturgical though it is) is greater than that of, say, the tonsure by which a man becomes a cleric.

Suggestions for further reading

Yves Congar, *Lay People in the Church* (Westminster, Md.: Newman, 1957); B. C. Butler, *The Idea of the Church* (Baltimore: Helicon, 1962); E. H. Schillebeeckx, *The Layman in the Church* (Staten Island: Alba House, 1963); K. H. Schelkle, *Discipleship and Priesthood* (New York: Herder and Herder, 1965); Hans Küng, *Structures of the Church* (New York: Nelson, 1964); ——— *The Church* (New York: Herder and Herder, 1968): a less technical summary of what Küng is offering in these two books may be found in his *The Council and Reunion* (New York: Sheed and Ward, 1961), pp. 188–214, and in his *The Living Church* (New York: Sheed and Ward, 1963), pp. 57–95, 333–369; J. L. McKenzie, *Authority in the Church* (New York: Sheed and Ward, 1966).

9. Christ, Church, and Sacrament

One of the most encouraging developments in current theology has been in writings on the sacraments. For too long our manual presentation of these has been without close reference either to the treatises on Christ or on the Church. They were considered as aids to grace, helps to our sanctification; there was a preoccupation with the *ex opere operato* formula which emphasized the built-in efficacy of the sacraments to the detriment of their need to be received in faith (it was difficult for those outside the Catholic Church to acquit us of a charge of quasi-magic). An essentialist philosophy behind our theology often showed itself: sacraments were like essences, "things," a view which obscured the dynamism of personal encounter with Christ which is now being called to our attention.

The writings of Eduard Schillebeeckx and Karl Rahner have done much to recall to us more worthy notions, and recent catechetical writings are filtering their sacramental theology through to the schools. The approach followed by each of these authors is somewhat different: Schillebeeckx from the standpoint of encounter theology, the sacraments being seen as decisive moments of encounter with Christ;

Rahner from the standpoint of the Church as the primordial sacrament who actualizes, makes present, develops her own inner being by the exercise of the sacraments. This difference of emphasis underlines two important girders underpinning any attempts at a treatise on the sacraments: christology and ecclesiology. Christ, Church, and sacrament must be viewed together.

The whole pattern of revelation as found in the Old and New Testaments is one of personal relationship, with God intervening personally in mankind's history, summoning man to respond to the salvation he was offering him. Along that whole history of salvation, challenging event and interpretative word marked the personal summons of God to the individual, demanding his decision. Revelation, the self-manifestation of God to man, was not to be found in any rarefied atmosphere of thought but in the inescapable events of day-to-day life (cf. chapter 3). But the ebb and flow of that history of salvation derived from man's wavering response to God. In a dialogue of personal freedom Jacob (Israel) wrestled with and resisted the God who calls. Only with that other representative of mankind, the man Jesus, was there to be found a perfect response to God. And in him that fidelity demanded by the covenant was realized in a twofold way: he is not only man's representative, responding to God — he is also the one sent, revealing God. From now on communion with God will be arrived at only through fellowship with our representative and God's revealer.

God is meeting us in a fully human way and our response to him must be fully human, the action of a person. Our encounter with him is not in some deep, mystic recess of the soul but through the body and the things of this world since the soul externalizes its process of becoming a person only in embodiment, through the flesh.

But if we are to meet God in the man Jesus, and if we are to respond to him via the human and the earthly to which we are tied — and not be satisfied with a spiritual or mental encounter — how can this now be effected? How can we come into contact with the saving events of Christ's life and death in a history that is now past and irrevocable? The historical Jesus is the exalted Christ.

We have to note that what is historical, what has taken place in time, is irreversible. Christ's human history cannot be made present to us even "in mystery." Yet because the passion, death, and resurrection of Christ were actions of a divine person they (like all things divine) are eternally present though the historical shape they took in human form is past. Further, Christ did not cease to be man after the resurrection: the New Testament was written precisely because of that joyful realization of the first Christians that Christ was the *living* Lord. If the eternally present divine redemption is to be made over to us, it can only be done through earthly things which symbolize the saving action of the historical Jesus and glorified Lord, man in both time and eternity.

CHURCH

It is here that the role of the Church in the economy of redemption must be introduced. Established to continue Christ's work, she exhibits in her very self some features of the incarnate Word: a visible, earthly appearance masks her invisible, divine task. She is the continuing sign of God's grace in the world and, like Christ, a primordial sacrament: "Christ is the historically real and actual presence of the eschatologically victorious mercy of God . . . the Church is the sign of the grace of God definitively triumphant in the world in Christ" (Rahner). The same author has expressed the relationship of the Church to Christ and to the sacraments in this way: "Viewed in relation to Christ, the Church is the abiding promulgation of his grace-giving presence in the world. Viewed in relation to the sacraments, the Church is the primal and fundamental sacrament" (*The Church and the Sacraments*, p. 201). And that permanent sign of grace in the world is for the whole world, not just for the members of the Church. The sacrifice of Christ was a "universal baptism" for all mankind; in him the whole human race became called, a "church."

But the Church, this sign of grace in the world, must make effective what she is, must actualize her nature. She must make over to men the personal saving act of the glorified and invisible Christ. This she does by her "sacramentalizing": in the ordinary matter supplied by man, itself lifeless and impotent, the glorified Christ effects through his Church, by virtue of his saving word, the divine mystery of salvation. The once-for-all, yet eternally present, redeeming action of the incarnate Word is thus given a public and visible place in men's lives, in the life of the individual who thus encounters his Lord as person-to-person. Through the ritual action of the Church in liturgical unity with the sacramental word, her own nature is externalized, made actual. The redemptive content of the past acts of the historical Jesus via the present saving action of the glorified Lord is now realized through the sacramental Church. And in all cases the human nature of Christ is involved.

SACRAMENT

When we come to look at the workings of the sacraments themselves a certain number of points arise. There is, first of all, the question of the causality of the sacraments. Our textbooks have discussed physical causality (the positing of a physical action — e.g., washing — brings about a physical effect), moral causality (the sacraments make a claim by intercession on God's grace), juridical (a sacrament confers a legal title to grace). But precisely because the sacraments are signs, should not their causality be seen as deriving from the very nature of a sign? Here we find that intrinsically real signs — as distinct from those called into play arbitrarily and by convention — indicate and make present something distinct from themselves. The body signifies and actualizes the soul; a human gesture signifies and deepens an interior human attitude; a person, through his body, indicates himself and becomes more fully what he is. Thus also the sacraments: they bring to pass what they signify. Through that encounter with Christ in the Church they signify the conferring of grace, and in actualizing the Church's potential of grace, they transmit it. The sacramental sign is cause of grace in that grace is conferred by being signified.

This actualization of the nature of the Church as God's sign of grace in the world is unfolded or articulated according to a number of rites. We speak of "seven" sacraments, but as long as we maintain that each of the Church's seven rites confers grace it is immaterial whether we speak of "six" sacraments (joining baptism and confirmation into one act of initiation) or of "nine" (separating the grades of deacon and bishop within orders). In this manner that general grace which is common to all the sacraments receives an intrinsic specialization in individual sacraments; there is, in the different rites, a dynamism directed to particular aspects of human and personal life. Besides those everyday actions which go to make up life for all of us, there are decisive moments which challenge a person more and call for a greater expression of one's responsibility. The sacraments cater to the high points of our Christian existence, those moments of marked personal decision which, in turn, influence the more humdrum aspects of that Christian living.

Because the institution of a sacrament can follow from the fact that Christ founded a Church with a sacramental nature, there is no need for us to search the Scriptures for words and deeds of Christ instituting seven sacraments. Indeed we shall search in vain for such sayings on confirmation, matrimony, orders, the anointing of the sick, whereas for baptism, the eucharist, and the forgiveness of sin the New Testament expressly states the commission of Christ to perform these rites. (One can understand Protestant reluctance to admit more than baptism and the eucharist; the words of Matthew, chapters 16 and 18 on "binding and loosing" are interpreted in a nonsacramental fashion.)

Another question is that of *opus operatum*. The common-place view that grace is conferred on the recipient through the positing of the sacramental sign itself, neither the holiness of the minister nor of the recipient being causally involved, has tended to soft-pedal the fact that receptiveness in faith of the grace conferred is also expressly taught by Trent. Because the Church is God's definitive sign in the world of his saving grace, those acts of the Church which realize her nature cannot of themselves fail. Here is the primary meaning of *opus operatum*: the putting into effect of the abiding and irrevocable promise of God for the individual human being. The previous view mentioned is only a secondary and negative formulation.

If one should inquire how the sacraments differ from those other, even official, prayers of the Church (e.g., the reading of Scripture), it has to be pointed out that both require due dispositions in the recipient and to both is grace promised. But only in the sacraments is there that indestructible and visible expression of God's consenting to answer man. The summons to grace and its sign are inseparable. Whereas in the prayers of the Church, in her sacramentals, there is something destructible, fragile, replaceable. There is not the same divine commitment as in those acts of the Church which actualize her nature. (Similarly, in the "sacraments of nature" of pagan ritual, even in the Old Testament, God was also really conferring grace on man, but without that underpinning by these effective signs that are the Church's sacraments.)

Opus operatum does not stand in opposition to faith: God, out of pure generosity, gives this faith and summons to man in the historical, visible forms of the sacraments. In fact it is through faith that the individual is brought within the sphere of the Church's action, accepting that summons made to him. Should those signs be posited without the due dispositions of the subject and so be impeded in their effect at that moment, they may still accomplish that effect later.

This "reviviscence" does not mean their coming to life again but rather that a sacramental sign works within the span of time in which, from the nature of the sign, the proffer of grace is able to continue. The sign of a "meal" (eucharist) is of shorter duration than the state of life entered into by baptism, orders, matrimony. And even when a sacrament is perhaps unfruitful at the moment of reception, still, in a certain way, it is not *completely* unfruitful because of its value as a sacramental prayer of Christ and his entire Church (cf. E. Schillebeeckx, "The Sacraments: an encounter with God," in *Christianity Divided*, p. 268).

This brings us to a final point which has been stressed by Schillebeeckx: the sacraments as mysteries of worship and sanctification. The redemptive act of Christ is essentially one of obedient love and adoration of the Father, shown on a created level. His redemptive act is a mystery of worship and in this he is our representative. At the same time Christ is working in us the effects of his redemption, sanctifying us. There is, then, worship and sanctification in the sacraments. Every sacrament is a sacramental prayer for *this* believer who now presents himself. To the prayer of Christ the Church joins her own prayer to the Father. Christ and his Church surround the recipient with prayer and he enters more deeply into that living bond which the community of the Church has with the mystery of Christ's flesh.

Fr. Schillebeeckx (*ibid.*, pp. 271–272) gathers together the various threads of his sacramental theology in a short passage that pinpoints its practical as well as theoretical aspects:

This sanctifying act of worship of the glorified high priest in heaven, sacramentalized in and through the Church, is *directed essentially* to that particular man in whom the sacrament is performed (consideration being made for the unique character of the eucharist as sacrifice of the Church and for the entire Church). This is so completely true that this personal involvement is part of the very essence of the sacrament. . . . However, this sanctifying sacramental mystery of worship of Christ in and through his Church can only develop *ex opere operato* all the rich fecundity for which it was established when the subject for whom the sacrament is intended also actively enters with a religious spirit into this mystery of worship with faith and an earnest longing for grace. Thus it will also become the sacramental expression of his personal desire to encounter Christ in faith.

Such a vital participation by the recipient in the sacraments will make for a more interior personal communion with Christ, a closer bond with the Church's community of grace and, consequently, an increased intimacy with Father, Son, and Spirit.

Suggestions for further reading

K. Rahner, *The Church and the Sacraments* (New York: Herder and Herder, 1963); E. H. Schillebeeckx, *Christ the Sacrament* (New York: Sheed and Ward, 1963); Otto Semmelroth, *Church and Sacrament* (Notre Dame, Ind.: Fides, 1965); C. O'Neill, *Meeting Christ in the Sacraments* (Staten Island: Alba House, 1965).

10. The Seven Sacraments

The last chapter dealt with some of the general considerations governing sacramental theology: how a sacrament is not so much a "thing" as a decisive meeting with Christ; how it is an actualization of the nature of the Church which is the sign of God's grace present in the world; how a sacrament renders present, publicly, and in a visible way, the eternal redeeming action of the incarnate Word by which the Father is worshiped and men sanctified. True though this may be, in the concrete that meeting, actualization, and worship with sanctification is found only in the acceptance of grace and the achievement of personal holiness by the individual Christian in his reception of each sacrament. Grace is not found *in vacuo*.

In the following brief considerations of the seven sacraments, emphasis will be laid on the christological, ecclesial, and religious aspects with some indication of the problems attached to the different sacraments. It should be pointed out that the grouping of sacraments into those "of the living" and those "of the dead" has receded before the more decisive grouping into sacraments which confer a character and those which do not. Baptism, confirmation, and orders bestow a character on the recipient, giving him a particular commission and its corresponding grace in the Church. No mere external thing, it seals the person in the depths of his being. This character is specifically an ecclesial effect of the sacrament: a commission in the Church. However the other sacraments, by establishing a particular relationship to the visible Church, also exhibit an ecclesial effect. The religious effect of the sacraments, which is more directly related to God and Christ, is that grace conferred by each sacrament.

BAPTISM

We are aware of how the notion of washing away original sin with its imagery has too often diverted attention from the profounder significance of this sacrament. The more primitive practice of immersion conveyed a better idea: the catechumen is immersed in the death of Christ, dies with him to this world, to rise with Christ to a new existence in a new creation. Immersion is a symbol of death but water, in its biblical precedents, is also the symbol of life. The baptized enters into a new life of incorporation into Christ by means of an external rite performed by the Church: he is incorporated into Christ by being incorporated into the Church. In both the Old and New Testaments the first subject of redemption is the people of God with whom God established his covenant and to whom he gave his promise. The individual achieves his salvation by belonging to that people; he cannot be party to the covenant all by himself. By baptism a person adheres in faith to the sacred community of the Lord and his baptism is a public witness, a proclamation, of his acceptance of the Church with her life and belief.

This initiation into the Church is also a sign, a sacramentum, of the other effects that follow from baptism. Through the character received in baptism the Church has an express and enduring claim on this person. Consecrated as a member of God's people, he is molded into the mystery of Christ, configured with him, given the gift of the Spirit, and sanctified for the worship of the Father with Christ. Because the Church continues the functions of Christ the members initiated by baptism share in his triple role of prophet, priest, and king.

Accustomed as we are to baptism being conferred in infancy we may find it strange that this practice is challenged by a number of non-Catholic theologians (an old controversy is being revived). But does not that adherence in faith required of the recipient in his personal decision to follow Christ demand a moral consciousness and evaluation that cannot be found in a child? Nevertheless, a community can accept an individual into itself without that individual being yet able to formalize acceptance. The Church can introduce into herself those still not capable of making a conscious response to Christ. The Church with her faith in Christ can still be the assurance of God's redeeming love toward those who have no knowledge of it. The time comes when such a person has to ratify that acceptance for himself, just as he has to ratify his own existence and belonging to humanity.

For those who die unbaptized we have postulated a baptism of desire. Too frequently we have limited this to catechumens who die before the actual conferring of the sacrament or to those who have more generally desired to be Christians. But it may not be too outrageous to suggest that God's saving grace is working on those who, without any clear knowledge of him, of Christ, and of his Church, attempt to follow, even falteringly, the dictates of their conscience. They in fact — even if they never formulate it as such — do will to be the recipients of God's saving grace. And for them as for unbaptized infants there is no need to erect a limbo: they have been included in that universal baptism of the Cross for all humanity and in the moment of their death they will be able to ratify personally their inclusion into Christ's own death for all.

CONFIRMATION

We are used to seeing this sacrament as that in which we receive the Holy Spirit for an apostolate of defense: we are made "soldiers of Jesus Christ." But confirmation is much more than this; it is instituted for more than the personal care of the individual soul. It is rather the charismatic sealing by a character which permits and indeed commissions a person to share in the mission and witness of the Church before and to the world, an extension of Christ's own function of prophet.

The question has been posed as to the relationship between baptism and confirmation, and non-Catholic answers have varied, some believing that it is *ad esse* of Christian initiation, others only *ad bene esse*, while a third group proposes that confirmation is an optional extra. Now in the baptismal sharing in Christ's death, with the baptized being taken out of this world of law and sin, a descent, there is incorporation into Christ's saving mystery and the Spirit is received. But there must be a sharing too in Christ's incarnation with its acceptance of the world with a view to its transfiguration and healing: a mission. The mighty sway and influence of the Spirit in the world is to be made effective through *this* Christian who is called to an ever greater incorporation into Christ and his mission. Because this completes the process of initiation and includes specific graces to sanctify a person in view of his mission, it must be expressed by a sacramental sign, in conjunction with, or separate from, the rite of initiation. The Church at Pentecost experienced the coming of the Spirit and her nature is such that that experience of the Spirit, which endowed her with charismatic gifts, must be actualized in her members.

This is not a question of one giving of the Spirit in baptism and a second coming in confirmation. Rather, that particular grace which constitutes a person as full member of the Church with a share in the Church's mission to the world demands that such a conferring of mission and grace be shown externally and publicly by sacramental rite. Such a rite is seen in the Acts of the Apostles: the imposition of hands. This vocation of mission to the world which brings with it the gifts of the Spirit will show itself differently in different individuals, and these gifts or charisms should not be defined by their more spectacular manifestations recorded in the New Testament, though even 1 Corinthians lists quite unexciting gifts. Prophecy is still powerful in the Church in the witness to Christ by her members through their daily living and their contribution to the development of her doctrine in which both hierarchy and laity participate.

EUCHARIST

The continuing liturgical changes as well as recent theological discussions on this sacrament — questions as to the Mass being both sacrifice and the Lord's Supper, as to how the Real Presence may be philosophically clarified, on "thanksgiving" and reservation, etc. — focused attention on aspects of eucharistic theology which, though important, do not always sound the depths of the sacrament so absolutely central to the Church's being. Karl Rahner (*Church and the Sacraments*, pages 84–85) tried to describe what the eucharist is to the Church by seeing as gathered together in the eucharist the various threads making up the fabric of the Church:

> For here everything that goes to form the Church is found fully and manifestly present: her separation from the world (even today this demands and justifies a sort of discipline of the secret, *disciplina arcani*); her hierarchical structure (priest and people); her attitude of dutiful receptivity to God, which forbids her to be an end in herself (sacrifice); her recitation of the efficacious words which render present what they proclaim (the *anamnesis*, the words of commemoration are the primal constitutive words of the Church); her unity (the one bread of which all eat in the sacred meal which unites all who take part in it); her expectation of the final kingdom, the glory of which is ritually anticipated in this celebration; her penitential spirit in offering the sacrifice which was offered

for the sin of the world: *donum paenitentiae concedens*; the invincibility of the grace of God, which was definitively given her, that she might be holy, for she has him who is the final victory and she already celebrates in advance the ultimate victory of God's kingdom, in the consciousness that she will do that until he comes again (1 Cor 2:26); her profound readiness to serve others (the sacrifice to God *pro totius mundi salute*).

Thus it is that the Church universal is present in her most intensive form in any local celebration of the eucharist. In partaking of the one Bread the communicant achieves a deeper incorporation into the Church and the whole range of her saving activity and thus achieves a deeper incorporation into Christ. A past event becomes a present experience and a future hope.

PENANCE

It may not be too exaggerated to suggest that in this sacrament legalism found an early and an easy prey: a minute counting of sins, rigid cross-examination, formalized protestation of sorrow, and an exact carrying out of the "penance." All of this tended to distract the penitent from concentration on the utterly basic requirement, repentance. There is more emphasis now on this need, more appreciation of how sin is to be measured by personal rejection of God rather than by tabulating do's and don'ts, even if such a rejection must show itself in actions. There is also an underlining of the necessity for conversion and repentance within biblical perspectives in the growing number of bible services and "group confessions." These latter stress the individual penitent's reconciliation with God and the Church but as a member of a penitent community.

And in fact in the sacrament of penance there is (once more) an actualization of the Church's nature. In the contrite penitent is manifested the Church herself as the penitent Church of sinners, bathing the feet of Christ with her tears, and yet a sign — an effective sign — of God's mercy to a world tied to sin. The Church must react against sin by which a member of her holy community puts himself in opposition to God and to the Church: she draws away from him. The mystery of sin has both an individual aspect and an ecclesial one by which the sinner must be reconciled, not only with God but also with the Church — but through the Church. And the acts of the penitent confessing to the Church are part of the sacramental sign itself; the sinner and the Church go to make up that sign of merciful grace that is conferred.

Now in this returning to God in faith and sorrow, sin is forgiven. But the complex layers that go to form a human person, the stages of disintegration sin has left in its wake, the distance created between us and God by our rejection of him — all these ensure that our total reconciliation with God must needs be a long drawn out process, and a very painful one. The effects of sin — the temporal punishment due to sin after the sin has been forgiven — are only gradually removed. In this task of total reconciliation the Church joins with her penitent member, pleading before God with Christ. This special prayer of the Church has, in the past, been presented under the notion of indulgences. Unfortunately legalism entered here and we became accustomed to viewing indulgences as a sort of credit system drawn on the Church's "treasury." Besides other obvious abuses, many too often forget that an indulgence was an extension of the sacrament of penance: the prayer of the Church for their total reconciliation, and that this total reconciliation demanded their cooperation in the painful process of belonging completely to God. Formal completion of the requirements for gaining an indulgence monopolized what should have had pride of place — penance.

ORDERS

Protestant (if not Anglican) exegesis and theology understand the apostolic office almost exclusively as ministry of the word, with the whole Church alone holding a commission for priestly ministry deriving from the universal priesthood of all baptized. Rudolf Bultmann has expressed it thus: "The community has no need of persons of special quality, that is, of priests, to mediate between the community and God" (*Theology of the New Testament*, p. 117). In an earlier chapter, "The Church in her Structure," we outlined the modern discussion on ecclesiastical office and it will be sufficient here to state that there has to be in the Church, not only an apostolic succession of institutions and doctrine, but also an apostolic succession in ministry, to ensure those institutions and that teaching.

That this is a sacrament can be shown from the fact that those called to the Church's ministry need a special grace of state to fulfill their sacred commission. "The character of order, the commission in the Church to the priesthood of authority, by the fact that it confers an official status also sanctifies the person, provided the recipient does not oppose the sanctity bestowed upon him" (Schillebeeckx, *Christ the Sacrament*, p. 216). And indeed, a ministry that is impious throughout is incompatible with a holy Church since God willed that the Church should be holy not only in essence, in her being, but also in her existence, in her daily living. The holiness of the Church is necessarily present in the ministry as a whole, but each minister, to whom is entrusted Word and Sacrament to be exercised in faith and love, must accept that grace and holiness for himself. Thus primed, as it were, for his function, in turn the exercise of his office is the irreducible means of his own sanctification: "The holiness of the priest is the living assimilation of his office, made possible by grace" (Rahner).

MATRIMONY

Recent studies have directed attention to two aspects of marriage which have merited more attention than has previously been given them: its mystery or sacramentalism and its personalism. Basic to marriage is the deep, personal love-relationship of husband and wife, and the acts of physical love shown in marriage become completely disorientated when isolated from that personal relationship. Even to consider those acts as legitimate only in view of procreation is to deny them their function of expressing the love of man and wife. Such concrete physical acts, then, hide a deeper dimension — the love of two persons.

But marriage itself has a real capacity to represent God's love in Christ for the mankind he created and called to salvation through covenant, incarnation, and Church. This is no mere representation or comparison but a facet of reality: the objective presence of personal love in the order of redemption. Christ's sacrifice of love, founding the Church, postulates the response of love from the human side, from each member. That foundation has taken into account the structure of the general human condition. In the sacrament of matrimony, the Church manifests herself as the mystery of the union between Christ and mankind since man and wife are joined together in a human love that has been raised to its true and supernatural level. No wonder, then, Ephesians 5 should dwell on the union of husband and wife as signifying and deriving from that more profound union of Christ and his Church. In a secular reality we have a saving mystery. Finally marriage contributes to the union of Christ and the Church in that it establishes miniature, but none the less genuine, communities of the redeemed, the human basis of the local Church.

In all this the grace of the sacrament of matrimony plays an immense role and it is only where such grace is thwarted that God's continuing plan for mankind is impeded, Christ's union with the Church obscured, and the growth of husband and wife in nature and grace stunted.

ANOINTING OF THE SICK

The supreme earthly reality of death itself becomes, with

Christ and the Church, a saving mystery also. Death summons each individual to decide about the ultimate meaning of existence. The Church is at hand here to support with the saving grace of hope the Christian who, from the worldly point of view, should be committed to negation and despair. Once more the Church actualizes her nature by showing how her eschatological expectation, her hope of final transfiguration in Christ, is able to transcend this world and the limits of sense, and this hope she communicates in grace to her suffering member. The perspectives are no longer the death of another Adam but the second coming of Christ to this member of the Church.

Death, then, becomes not a passive acquiescence in human mortality but the last deeply personal surrender to Christ which was initiated by baptism, sealed by the Spirit in confirmation, prepared for in every partaking of the Lord's Supper (itself a temporary measure "till he comes"), repaired by penance, undergirded by the ministry of the Church, symbolized in the loving dedication of marriage.

Suggestions for further reading

Charles Davis, *Sacraments of Initiation: baptism and confirmation* (New York: Sheed & Ward, 1964); *Sacraments: the gestures of Christ*, ed. D. O'Callaghan (New York: Sheed & Ward, 1965); *Sacraments in Scripture*, ed. T. Worden (Springfield, Ill.: Templegate, 1966); *Church and Eucharist*, ed. M. Hurley (Dublin: Gill, 1966); H. J. Richards, P. De Rosa, *Christ in our World: a study of baptism, the eucharist, penance, and matrimony* (Milwaukee: Bruce, 1966); J. P. Schanz, *The Sacraments of Life and Worship* (Milwaukee: Bruce, 1966); F. J. Heggen, *Confession and the Service of Penance* (London: Sheed & Ward, 1967).

11. The Last Things

If there is one section of our theology textbooks which is crying out to be demythologized, to be freed from the shackles of early mythological and apocalyptic thought forms and descriptions, it is "The Last Things." Poor exegesis has given us signs of approach of the end of the world like the return of Henoch and Elijah; psychedelic hallucinations of that end abound, as well as of the last judgment, of hell, of the condition of the damned; theological speculation is too often ruggedly fundamentalist in its employment of Scripture texts — though it has to be admitted that our New Testament writers cannot easily be acquitted of the charge that they themselves believed in the panorama enveloping their teaching.

This question of the "four last things" has to be put into the wider framework of the final consummation of all creation, the study of "eschatology." Admittedly until somewhat recently even this term was confined to the study of death, judgment, hell, and heaven. R. H. Charles could subtitle his massive study of eschatology: "A Critical History of the Doctrine of a Future Life." Today there is a different and wider connotation. The word still includes all that Charles understood by the term but it also reminds us that "this life which we live here on earth is itself significant for eternity, and that eternity is actually shaped and moulded by the purpose of God as that purpose works out in this life that we know here and now" (George Knight, A Christian Theology of the Old Testament, p. 240). Devotional literature used to be peppered with warnings about the "latter days," the prelude to the end of the world, but in fact, since the coming of Christ — God's final and decisive intervention in human history — we are living in those latter days between the Passover and the Parousia.

Eschatology has been recently described as "the storm center of theology," as "one of the most burning questions in New Testament theology" due to the revolutionary changes in perspectives. We can distinguish two schools of thought in this matter of interpreting the New Testament data. There are those who see history moving toward its final climax and consummation without any further invasion of God. Others prefer to believe that history will be brought to a close by such a divine intervention.

Within these views the fate of the individual, of the community, and of the cosmos have to be considered. There are those whose eschatology is futuristic: there will be a final dissolution in some indefinite future (usually at a great remove from our times) with, however, an interim judgment on the individual soul at death. This view has been standard enough but it has the disadvantage of employing the mythological and apocalyptic forms just referred to. Further, it can serve (as did apocalyptic) as an escape hatch into another world from the sufferings and oppressions of this life. Others, recalling St. John's references to "the hour comes and now is," accept a realized eschatology: the promised events are already taking place. Men, by their present actions, are already judging themselves; eternal life is in some way a present possession. This approach has the advantage that the last things become meaningful now. Yet, because of the emphasis on the individual, there is a neglect of that expectation of the community and of the cosmos which have such importance in the New Testament. All references, too, to the future are not omitted by John and there is the insistence from the Synoptists on the future kingdom.

It has been proposed that creation, redemption, and consummation should be seen as three aspects of one eternal act of God. The doctrine of creation as found in the Bible need not be taken as primarily concerned with a beginning of the world but rather with the beginning of God's purpose for man: man and the world are dependent upon him. This purpose was worked out through Christ. Similarly, eschatology need not be primarily concerned with an end of the world but rather with the fact that man and the world are destined to find completion and consummation in God through Christ. In Christ the whole universe is moving toward its final perfection, with redemption covering both man and nature. With his exaltation as Lord, Christ's role assumed cosmic proportion and his function has been to integrate all mankind and creation into union with himself as his *pleroma*, his fullness. It is obviously extremely difficult to define closely this New Testament notion of a *pleroma*, of the body of Christ come to full perfection. Opinions have run the gamut from "mystical identification" to an uncompromising physical reality which, it is claimed, is nothing less than what is envisaged by St. Paul. What we can be sure of is a transfiguration of man and the world through Christ. And in this transfiguration of man and the cosmos, the consummation of all things, lies the ultimate self-revelation of Christ in his cosmic role — his second coming or parousia and the "general judgment" of mankind. In his *Theological Dictionary* (under the entry Judgement) Karl Rahner writes:

> The Judgement must be seen in the context of the consummation of the world and of history as a whole. It will then be clear that those NT texts which closely connect the Judgement with the parousia . . . are part of our basic information about the Judgement. This consummation is called the Judge-

ment of God because on the one hand the radical disclosure
of the completion of all the history of the world that has
been enacted in freedom is central to it, and on the other
hand the consummation is not simply the result of a development immanent in the world, but depends on the sover-
eign discretion of God (an end that is fixed, not merely
arrived at). This consummation is called the Judgement of
Christ because its ultimate character is essentially determined
by the nature and work of Christ — this on account of the
Christocentrism of all reality in all its dimensions. Because
it comes upon all (in the framework of their interrelations,
consummating both good and evil) it is called the general
Judgement. Because it is the final consummation which ter-
minates history it is called the Last Judgement.

THE FOUR LAST THINGS

When we move from these general considerations of eschatology to the more particular ones of death, judgment, hell,
and heaven, we shall find that there has been new thinking
on traditional positions by a number of Catholic scholars.
Ladislaus Boros, in The Mystery of Death, has reviewed
several of these investigations while adding considerably to
the new hypothesis — and it is only an hypothesis — on the
theology of death.

In the first place, death itself is not to be seen in terms
of a mere biological occurrence but in terms of a personal
act which is the climax of an individual's life. A human
person is continually in a state of becoming. The process
begins at conception and is maintained during the whole
period of his earthly existence. As long as man was regarded
as an essentially static being, established in the fullness of
his personality from birth with his daily activity only an
accidental addition to his nature, death could be no more
than an earthly termination of that activity. Now, however,
death can be seen as the high point in this process of becoming, the supreme personal act of an individual, an exercise of that freedom and responsibility inherent in the notion of a "person." Only now, we are told, can the perfect

and full exercise of personal freedom be achieved. Man in death is in complete self-possession and is now capable of expressing and of disposing of himself totally and definitively: the final act in his task of realizing himself.

The mechanics of this situation are explained thus to us. The soul leaving the body awakens to its pure spirituality (others dispute such a state, see below), understands its life, and is confronted with the universe illumined by Christ. There is an encounter with Christ in which the individual must choose either for or against him. The radical freedom of God's creature, the ultimate domain in man, will not be interfered with by Christ. This encounter takes place in the very moment of death itself — not before, when one is in the throes of the last agony, not afterward when eternity is fixed. This decisive personal choice in death explains the "particular judgement" as being essentially this decision itself. (Even during life man is judging himself in his attitude toward Christ, a point insisted upon in the Fourth Gospel.) We may note, too, how the New Testament sees in death the coming of the Lord, the manifestation of Christ.

This hypothesis, besides taking into account a deeper understanding of man, shows a greater appreciation of the universal salvific will of God: the countless millions who have never been reached by the Christian message do, in that moment of death, possess the possibility of making a free and personal decision for Christ, who has in fact redeemed them but who awaits their personal ratification. There is no need, consequently, to postulate a "limbo" for good pagans who have been considered as being too good for hell and too bad for heaven! Pace Ronald Knox, there are no border-line cases in eternity.

The notion of "purgatory" is also covered by this encounter with Christ in death. Rather than as a state lasting a longer or shorter duration, it may be conceived of in terms of intensity, linked to the quality of the decision accomplished in death. A purification of self, a rejection of all that stands between us and Christ, is involved in this meeting with him. The renunciation of the dregs of sin and self in this final loving surrender to Christ would occasion suffering of a greater or less intensity depending on how radical such a renunciation must be. And that is why we cannot write off as irrelevant, in view of this possibility of a choice in death, the good or evil we do in life. It may be difficult for us to envisage how a person meeting Christ could reject him. Yet our full freedom remains and it is not inconceivable that rejection of Christ could be preferred to renunciation of a self that has been constituted into the goal of one's existence, another god. The Church prays for the dead that in this encounter with Christ the individual may accept in full freedom the grace of salvation he is offering him.

Consequent on this decision for or against Christ one's eternity is fixed, hell or heaven. It should be clear from what has been said that it is not a question of God condemning a person to hell but rather of this person freely choosing, totally and definitively, to reject Christ. It is a self-judgment, an affirmation of the whole person against Christ. Hell should not be seen as a punishment for past sins, perhaps now bitterly rejected, but as an enduring attitude of rejection of Christ's love: an affirmation of sin as such. The will of the damned is not to love God; that is their hell. St. John speaks of those who are not judged because they have believed, thus accepting Christ; those who do not believe, who do not accept Christ, are already judged.

This deliberate separation from God produces a twofold discord: an inner conflict which comes from this that the inescapable relationship each of us has to God is now joined to an inescapable and eternal godlessness (the poena damni, the pain of loss, of the theologians); there is also in the damned a state of hostility to the universe and to all that is in it (poena sensus, of suffering). The universe bears the stamp of the God who created it and man forms part of that universe. The damned find themselves in conflict with all that surrounds them and which afflicts them in the depths of their being. Bishop Robinson has spoken of hell as union in estrangement with the Ground of our being. The damned are eternal misfits.

We shall search in vain to locate hell (and heaven): the geography of the next world belongs to a Christian mythology rather than to the Christian message. Yet hell and heaven are more than states. We can speak of a "place" in an analogous sense to mean the social dimension of the next life. Heaven includes a fellowship among the blessed and hell the company of the damned.

While hell is a twofold discord, heaven is a twofold harmony: union in happiness with God and with his creation, nature and man. The moment of truth, when the individual encountered Christ, opened out into eternal knowledge and love. And this knowledge and love embrace the whole of the universe which was reconciled to God in Christ's death and transfigured with him in his exaltation.

RESURRECTION

One final question needs to be mentioned in connection with the newer perspectives on the last things — the resurrection of the body. We are accustomed to that presentation of this doctrine which states that on the last day all will rise from the dead, the soul being once more joined to the identical body it informed during this life but which, in the resurrection, has been glorified if heaven has been merited.

Some points call for reconsideration. We are accustomed, from Aristotelian philosophy, to the Greek notion of a clean-cut separation of body and soul, with the soul being the immortal and continuing part of man (Hebrew thought does not seem to envisage such a duality). Our theology took over the Greek distinction and separation of body and soul, affirming the immortality of the soul and the resurrection of the flesh, and allowing, seemingly, a period between death and its separation of body and soul and the reassumption by the soul of the body in the resurrection.

But in the doctrines proposed by the Church on the immortality of the soul and the resurrection of the flesh, the whole man in his unity is always meant: the resurrection of the flesh in the creed means the definitive salvation of man as a whole and the immortality of the soul is also concerned with such a life. The assertions are directed to the whole reality and meaning of man.

In the Middle Ages we find several pronouncements of the magisterium stating that man can attain the full happiness of God not merely on the last day but immediately after death. Such affirmations were made in the contemporary debate about "separated souls," but the debate was basically concerned with whether or not man could see God immediately after death, and not with the precise constitution of man at that stage — pure soul or in some way corporeal. It has recently been proposed that after death the soul does not continue to exist entirely "separately," without any corporeality. Man, it is suggested, is corporeal in a certain way from the moment of his entry into eternal bliss: he is ready to rise immediately after death. It has been suggested, too, that the resurrection of the dead simply means the hope and conviction that in the end we shall be with God with our whole existence. There is no agreement in theological tradition about that aspect of bodily resurrection, identity of matter, and it is quite an open question whether anything at all is to be said on the point.

Suggestions for further reading

A. Winklhofer, *The Coming of His Kingdom* (New York: Herder and Herder, 1963); L. Boros, *The Mystery of Death* (New York: Herder and Herder, 1965).

12. A New Hermeneutics

Much of what has been discussed in the foregoing pages may seem to demand some justification in principle. Our opening chapters indicated three forces at work in the renewal of our theology: dialogue with the world, with other Christian churches, and among Catholic theologians themselves. Some attempt was then made to see how our theology has been able to integrate worthwhile contributions from these three sources. But has there not been some accommodation to secular forces, to non-Catholic views, to "fringe" theology in the Church itself? We are convinced that this has not been the case.

On questions touching man in nature and grace, on the relation of theology to culture, the postulates of modern science have simply been used to explicate the Christian message. The development of dogma happens precisely via attempts to situate the insights of different periods within the Church's teaching. There is a two-way traffic: the Church can assimilate secular advances and thus christianize them. The world can learn from her but she can also learn from the world. Yet in accepting what the world has to offer, the Church cannot demand an absolute. Progress in human knowledge effects modifications, reversals, rejections of earlier theories. If theology employs current thought patterns and language to express the Church's message, this is not to make that message dependent on such expressions. Wasn't it Pope John who reminded us of the distinction between the dogma and its formulation? Hence, for example, if evolutionary theories are being explored to throw light on the theological meaning of man's emergence and of original sin, it is not a question of theology capitulating to science but of "faith seeking understanding" — *fides quaerens intellectum*.

Again, the employment of Protestant insights on the Word of God in the Scripture, on faith as response to that Word, on the encounter between God and man may suggest that Protestant platitudes have been beaten into Catholic epigrams, that we are discovering freshly for ourselves things which, with Protestants, have now become familiar. But this is no reason for refusing to integrate into our theology such realizations of Christian truth and experiences of Christian living as are valid for the total Christian world. It is sheer bigotry to confine the workings of the Spirit of truth to the Catholic Church.

As to the restatement of our theology by Catholic theologians, this requires a fuller discussion since their impact on us is more immediate and, when all is said and done, it is through them that that triple dialogue reaches the faithful. This restatement of theology derives from a reinterpretation of the scriptural and doctrinal data which has been sparked off by that triple confrontation. This reinterpretation, a "new hermeneutics" if you like, may be examined, then, vis-à-vis exegesis and doctrinal statements.

DEMYTHOLOGIZING

We have already noted the modern understanding of the Scripture accounts of man's creation and fall. It is generally recognized that these accounts are dressed in a mythological form and it is the task of exegetes to separate the teaching of Genesis from that incidental presentation. For the rest of the Old Testament writings, these are to be seen as embodying external event and interior experience, which latter was described in the then contemporary literary forms. Often it is not so much history that we are getting in the Old Testament as history interpreted and applied to current preoccupations. Similarly in the New Testament, the Spirit helped tradition and the writers to see and record the deep significance of the events of Christ's life, and to report this meaning in terms familiar to the primitive community. We need not linger over how form criticism has made us aware of the different literary procedures adopted by the evangelists and their schools to promote their message: midrash (e.g., in the Infancy Narratives of Matthew and Luke), liturgical (e.g., the "Our Father" in Matthew), catechetical (e.g., the Sermon on the Mount), etc. But more recently there has been reconsideration of the world picture current in New Testament times and it is acknowledged that this has offered elements of presentation to its writers which may safely be separated from the essential message they were trying to convey.

Reinterpretation of the New Testament message along these lines — demythologizing — is valid within recognizable limits. We may recall some examples. A view of the universe as a three-storied structure situated heaven above and hell below the earth. Whence in Luke's description of the ascension we find Christ being borne skyward. We have to leave aside this primitive cosmology and interpret the episode as showing that Christ, by virtue of his resurrection, is with the Father. The ascension, the last of the post-resurrection apparitions, is a symbolic gesture. Similarly the expression "descended into hell" is made up of elements which contradict our knowledge of the universe and must be expressed in terms that mean something today. In saying Christ "descended into hell" we affirm that he really died.

In the New Testament world picture angels and demons proliferated. Is the existence of the angels a supposition based on Scripture's view of the world, or is it an actually revealed truth? We do find in the Old and New Testaments three occurring media for the communication of revelation: angels, dreams, and visions. (Sometimes we find both together, as when the angel appeared in a dream to Joseph.) Is the medium also part of the message, or simply a way of expressing a particular intervention of God? It has been suggested that the meaning of scriptural references to angels seems to be the truth that all things, visible and invisible, come from God; that he does communicate with man; and that he is concerned for us in a thousand ways. The Nicene Creed speaks of God as "creator of all things visible and invisible," as does also the Fourth Lateran Council of 1215. But the point in question was that anything that exists is from God the creator — there is nothing which owes its existence to an evil principle (as was affirmed by the Manichean and Albigensian heresies). That Lateran Council was concerned to establish God's sovereignty in creation, not to define the existence of good or evil spirits, although it presupposes the terms of the contemporary debate. If it should be pointed out that angels figure prominently also in the liturgy we have to recall that the liturgy uses considerable biblical imagery without passing judgment as to its historical value: it does not always presume historical facts or real persons behind its references (we may think of its employment of descriptions from the Apocalypse on the heavenly Jerusalem, its references to Abel, Job, etc.).

As to demons, the Gospels do not show a distinction between being ill — particularly mentally ill — and being possessed. Matthew 17:15, for example, tells us that the boy tormented by a demon was "an epileptic." Christ saw something of Satan in these illnesses and spoke of him as a personal power. Was it a personification of evil, that horrifying evil which we see at work among men, often so much greater than individual malice? Karl Rahner has the following observations in his *Theological Dictionary* (under the entry Devils, Demons):

In view of the seriousness of saving history it would be un-theological levity to look on Satan and his devils as a sort of "hobgoblins knocking about the world"; rather it may be assumed that they are powers of the world insofar as this world is a denial of God and a temptation to man. This view preserves the personal nature of the devils, which is laid down by Scripture and the magisterium (D 2318), since every essential disorder in the world is personally realized; it also preserves their plurality, which is to be visualized in the context of the world's qualitative and regional plurality.

To sum up on angels and demons, we may say that their existence as personal beings in the sense in which we have been accustomed to think of them is an open question. God cares for us, and reveals himself to us, in a thousand ways. Yet there is an accumulative power of evil, showing itself in a horrifying fashion, among men. Are such manifestations of love, of evil, however, really spiritual beings?

Another New Testament field for demythologizing, we will recall, is those parts describing the end of the world and the last things. We have already touched upon death, judgment, hell, heaven, purgatory and limbo, the resurrection. The New Testament descriptions of the end of the world "depict in extremely vivid colours the calamities and miseries of all ages, the horrors of war, even catastrophes on a cosmic scale. . . . Hence they are not a description of the course of events at the end. They give us a general sense of the course of history and its consummation, affirming that whatever happens, God moves to his triumph in all things" (A New Catechism, Herder and Herder, 1967, p. 478).

It may be queried, did not the sacred authors believe in that world picture we find in the New Testament; is it not part of their teaching? We have to admit outright that they were children of their times and accepted contemporary cosmology and apocalyptic beliefs. It is a recognizedly valid procedure for exegetes to distinguish what the sacred writers intentionally taught from the literary form used to communicate that teaching. We may go further. We can distinguish what those authors taught and what they thought but did not teach. Since both we and they regard the Bible as a handbook of salvation, in practice the distinction lies between the teaching on the true redemptive relationship between God and man and any literary form or conceptual framework in which this is expressed.

NEW HERMENEUTICS FOR THEOLOGY

It must be evident from what has just been said that a reconsideration of the data of Scripture must lead to a reinterpretation of some traditional teaching and some outlines of this have been discussed in this book. But besides such a revaluation of the scriptural data, new insights from current thought must be employed to explicate the deposit of revelation. The Church's theologians throughout her history have performed this service and there is no reason why a halt to this process should be called for fear of contamination from the world. Further, theology has to make the Church's message meaningful to men of each succeeding period of her history which demands that some consideration must be given to their thought forms and language. We shall find that the central problem for the "new hermeneutics" in theology is that of formulation.

Every human statement, including dogmatic statements, is conditioned by the period in which it was made. There is first of all the *historical* situation which gave rise to it — in the case of dogmatic definitions, we find more often than not an attempt by the Church to ward off infiltrations from heretical or near-heretical sects which would damage the truth she is maintaining, even if as yet she possesses no conscious formulation of it. This protective attitude of the Church has often hardened (among theological schools) into an out-and-out polemic against those whose views had forced the Church to define her position. So not only have we to take into account, in assessing the relevant definition, the controversial point of issue but also the commentaries of theologians of the period who were often too prone to overemphasize Catholic affirmations to the detriment of soft-pedaling points of Catholic belief which their opponents insisted upon but in an isolated manner. It is extremely instructive to read Hans Küng's *Justification* to see on how many points Catholics and Protestants agree (there are marked divergences, of course) but which have become centers of dispute through a misreading of Trent and by polemics on both sides. The formulation of dogmas, then, owes much to the historical circumstances in which it arose and the formulation must be interpreted according to those circumstances. The *ad hoc* discussions preceding such a formulation are immensely important for delineating the sense and limits of that formula.

And even when the history behind the formula is ascertained, the *text* itself must be examined. Here one must distinguish what is introductory, what is doctrine, what is digression, what is the authentic meaning at stake, and whether this meaning is a statement of divine revelation or only something which is related to it. The demands inherent in such an analysis of a document of the *magisterium* are obviously formidable and it would be a rash theologian, indeed, who would presume to reach for his Denzinger to establish conclusively the sense of a definition. Textbooks have been known in the past to move in their successive editions from a *de fide* note to a thesis to a more humble *sententia communis* qualification.

Then the actual terminology employed in the document: how far is the Church committed to the *philosophy* from which the terms and the conceptual framework are borrowed? When Trent, for example, speaking of the conversion of the bread and wine into the body and blood of Christ, uses the terms "substance," "appearances" (*species*), "transubstantiation," did it not only borrow such terms from scholastic philosophy but even authenticate such concepts implied by those terms? We are all aware of the present controversy surrounding the notions of "transignification" and "transfinalization" as attempts to restate the traditional teaching on the presence of Christ in the eucharist.

Attempts to express a dogma defined in terms from another historical, philosophical, and linguistic context in a way that is meaningful to men of our time is an extremely delicate task, but nonetheless an urgent one. The words of Pope John are the charter for this:

> But from the renewed, serene, and tranquil adherence to all the teaching of the Church in its entirety and preciseness, as it still shines forth in the Acts of the Council of Trent and First Vatican Council, the Christian, Catholic and apostolic spirit of the whole world expects a step forward toward a doctrinal penetration and formation of consciousness in faithful and perfect conformity to the authentic doctrine, which, however, should be studied and expounded through the methods of research and through the literary forms of modern thought. The substance of the ancient doctrine of the deposit of faith is one thing, and the way in which it is presented is another. And it is the latter that must be taken into great consideration with patience if necessary, everything being measured in the forms and proportions of a magisterium which is predominantly pastoral in character.
>
> (Opening Speech to the Council, October 11, 1962)

We have already noted above (with reference to the New Testament) the distinction between the sacred authors' teaching on the true redemptive relationship between God and man and any literary form or conceptual framework in which this is expressed. The same may be said of the fathers in the various councils of the Church. We may even have to assert that, in some cases, we see where this distinction lies although the sacred authors or the council fathers did not.

Another point in this reinterpretation is that what is often presented as the "traditional teaching of the Church" is, in point of fact, something which is conventional rather than belonging to the true tradition of the Church. (A generation ago a fairly fundamentalist understanding of Genesis 1–11 would have been presented as the "traditional teaching.") Alfred Wikenhauser, in his *Introduction to the New Testament*, made an interesting distinction. He referred to "traditions *in* the Church" and "traditions *of* the Church." The latter must be maintained but the former are subject to rescrutiny and may lapse before the recognized and stable gains of research.

Finally, in a period of secularism with its assumption that this world, which comes increasingly under the control of man, is all that there is, when the area of basic religious phenomena of conversion, communion, the experience of sin and forgiveness, etc., are explained as mechanisms of the human psyche, it is imperative that theologians search the time-old teachings for further enlightenment. Karl Rahner has told us that past definitions are not the end of an affair but rather the starting point for renewed investigation, for further development. And this is more than ever necessary today. Dogmas are not merely words, they are values which enlarge our horizons. Grace and nature are interwoven, but this is not to deny that grace should clearly be seen as something which goes beyond nature: all the workings of grace cannot be expressed in terms of human perfectibility. The operation of grace and divine truth in all aspects of existence ensure that we shall be fully human, fully ourselves. It is these perspectives which our present theology must make clear. A task, but also a challenge.

Suggestions for further reading

K. Rahner, *The Church After the Council* (New York: Herder and Herder, 1966); J. Ratzinger, *Theological Highlights of Vatican II* (Glen Rock, N. J.: Paulist Press, 1966); B. C. Butler, *The Theology of Vatican II* (London: Darton, Longman and Todd, 1967).

Index

Adam, 32 ff
Adam, K., 15, 47
Allocutio of Paul VI to Vatican II, 53
Altizer, T., 8, 24
Angels, 94 ff
Anointing of the Sick, 82
Anonymous presence of God, 29
Anthropology, Christian, 7, 37 f, 50 f
Apostolate of the Laity, Decree on, 3, 57, 61
Apostolic succession, 63
Ascension of Christ, 94
Aubert, R., 38

Baillie, D. M., 46
Baptism, 75 f; Church and, 76; Confirmation and, 77 f; infant, 76; unbaptized babies, 76, 88
Barth, K., 12 f
Baum, G., 48
Bea, Card. A., 53
Biblical inerrancy, 18 f
Bishops, 57 ff; *Pastoral Office, Decree on,* 3, 57
Body, resurrection of, 90 f
Body-soul dualism, 90
Bonhoeffer, D., 7, 26
Boros, L., 87
Bouyer, L., 44
Brunner, E., 12 f
Bultmann, R., 7, 12 ff, 81

Catholic pacesetters in theology, 15 f
Causality of sacraments, 69 f
Changes in theology, disconcerting, 1 f
Character, sacramental, 74 f; of baptism, 75 f; of confirmation, 77 f; of orders, 64, 81
Charles, R. H., 84
Charisms, 52, 62
Christ: Church and sacrament, 66 ff; encounter with, 66 ff, 88 f; faith in, 41 ff; final consummation of all in, 86; incarnation, 36; incorporation into, 75; and Kingdom, 55;

Lord, 68, 86; matrimony and, 82; primordial sacrament, 68; redemption, 72; revealer and representative, 67, 72; surrender in faith to, 45 ff
Christian anthropology, 7, 37 f, 50 f
Christian churches, recognition by Vatican II, 10 f, 50 f
Christian message and secular realities, 7 f, 37 f
Christianity, religionless, 26, 29
Christology, functional, 14; lack of development in, v f
Church, and baptism, 76; Christ, sacrament and, 66 ff; clergy and laity in, 61; *Dogmatic Constitution on the,* 3, 48 ff, 57 ff, 60 f; eschatological holiness of, 53 f; Eucharist and the, 59, 78 f; hierarchical structure of, 48, 52; incarnational aspect of, 2, 4, 7, 38, 50 f, 69; images of, 48; local, 63 f, 79; and matrimony, 82; members of, 51; in *Modern World, Pastoral Constitution on,* 3, 4, 8, 10 f, 38, 50, 61; in her mystery, 48 ff; as Mystical Body, 47 ff, 50 f; people of God, 50 ff; prophetical, priestly, royal, 51 f, 59, 60 ff; pilgrims and sinners, 10 f, 52 ff, 79 f; primordial sacrament, 68 f; renewal in study of, 47 f; role of laity in, 61; service in, 57, 79; sign of God's presence in the world, 48 ff, 68 ff; structure of, 56 f; self-realization in sacraments, 51, 69 ff
Church and world, 4, 7 f, 30, 38, 50 f, 69
Clergy and laity, 61
Collegiality, episcopal, 58 f
Confirmation, sacrament of, 77 ff
Congar, Yves, 16, 49
Consecration, sacramentality of episcopal, 58
Consultation, of laity, 61; and *trina,* 64

101